The Proverb[s]
Handbook

*An Easy to Follow Daily Devotional
Explaining How to Be a "Proverbs 31 Wife"
in Today's Culture.*

Proverbs31WifeHandbook.com
By: Lara Velez, Founder of Moms of Faith

Credits:

Cover Art: Dreamstime.com
(Blue Hyacinth flower)

Note about Flower: Blue Hyacinth means "Constancy". Determination and consistency will be vital in this study.

This book is dedicated to my beloved husband, Robert. I love and appreciate you more than words can ever express. Thank you for your abundant patience, limitless support, daily encouragement and constant love.

I am my beloved's, And my beloved is mine...

- Song of Solomon 6:3

About the Author

Lara is a wife, mom, homeschooler, published author, ministry leader, speaker, and supreme multi-tasker! She is honest and forthright in her writing, and shares her heart, struggles, joys, pains, and the many lessons she has learned on her journey–in a relatable way that pulls no punches.

Besides all that, she is a chauffeur, friend, maid, chef, business owner, lover, confidant, mentor, teacher, seeker, nurse, boo-boo kisser, cat lover, coffee drinker, Starbucks follower, Mexican food addict, jean loving, sometimes loud mouth, opinionated, outspoken, web designer, iphone carrier, a teensy bit anal retentive, chocoholic, Survivor fan, Bible believing, animal lover, reptile and crawly things hating, speed walking, honest, working her way back to skinny jeans, and... One heck of a strong woman! (Among other things)

"O God, listen to my cry! Hear my prayer! From the ends of the earth, I cry to You for help when my heart is overwhelmed. Lead me to the towering rock of safety, for You are my safe refuge, a fortress where my enemies cannot reach me. Let me live forever in Your sanctuary, safe beneath the shelter of Your wings!" – Psalm 61:1-4

You can email her at:
contact@proverbs31wifehandbook.com

Be Blessed!

Table of Contents

Day 1: Introduction_____6

Day 2: Proverbs 31:10_____16

Day 3: Proverbs 31:11_____20

Day 4: Proverbs 31:12_____25

Day 5: Proverbs 31:13_____33

Day 6: Proverbs 31:14_____39

Day 7: Proverbs 31:15_____43

Day 8: Proverbs 31:16_____49

Day 9: Proverbs 31:17_____55

Day 10: Proverbs 31:18_____60

Day 11: Proverbs 31:19_____66

Day 12: Proverbs 31:20_____72

Day 13: Proverbs 31:21_____78

Day 14: Proverbs 31:22_____86

Day 15: Proverbs 31:23_____93

Day 16: Proverbs 31:24_____98

Day 17: Proverbs 31:25_____103

Day 18: Proverbs 31:26_____109

Day 19: Proverbs 31:27, part 1_____116

Day 20: Proverbs 31:27, part 2_____122

Day 21: Proverbs 31:27, part 3_____129

Day 22: Proverbs 31:28a_____134

Day 23: Proverbs 31:28b-29_____139

Day 24: Proverbs 31:30_____145

Day 25: Proverbs 31:31_____150

Day 26: Final Thoughts…_____155

My Testimony: the short version…_____157

Ongoing Support_____160

Day 1: Introduction

The sanctity of marriage is an area that is under a great deal of attack in our society. Everywhere you look there are gossip magazines and television shows telling of steamy affairs, separation, and divorce.

Common excuses are; I fell out of "love" with him/her, My life is going in a different direction, He/she wasn't meeting my needs...The list goes on. Unfortunately, Christians are just as likely to divorce as non-Christians. This should not be so. The Church has a responsibility to set an example to the world we live in.

How?

First, we must realize that God's design for marriage is the opposite of what the world's idea of marriage is. He compares marriage with Christ and the Church. Christ as the husband and the Church as His bride.

Divorce was never intended...

In Malachi 2:16 God tells us that He hates divorce and marital separation. He designed marriage to be two separate individuals becoming one, and remain strong in Him.

Please, don't get me wrong...God loves us, and when we do divorce, He forgives us. However, that does not give us the green light to just ignore His ways. He gave us specific instructions on how to have a happy marriage in Ephesians 5:20-33. The problem is that we allow our flesh to get in the way. If we do not get what we want, or things don't happen when "we" think they should, or we choose to disobey God's instructions for marriage, divorce becomes a viable option. That should not be so. Divorce should not even be an option--period.

I have been through a lot in my own marriage and have overcome many obstacles that would warrant divorce in the eyes of the world. We have been through separation, infidelity, loss and abuse. Many lessons were learned along the way. It is only by God's grace that we made it through the very dark times in our marriage.

One thing that is never considered anymore is divorce. It is not an option. We are in this through thick and thin, good and bad, pain and joy. We are married for *life*.

When we choose to take on that mentality, it really does help. It puts things in perspective and allows us to realize forgiving is our only option. Forgiveness is HUGE. I strongly believe that forgiveness is the *only* way anyone can have a long lasting marriage. One cannot expect to spend a lifetime with someone and never experience betrayal, disappointments and pain. When we come to a place where we *choose* to not allow divorce to be an option and *forgive* as we are forgiven, we may just find ourselves in an awesome marriage! Nothing should be labeled "unforgivable". All things, yes *all* things, are possible through Christ and with mercy and forgiveness! (I am speaking from experience.)

Before we begin this journey, I want urge you to shake off the world's views and ideas of the culture in regards to marriage. Then, open your mind and heart to what the Word of God says about it.

I also want you to forget what your husband "should" be doing and submit to God's Will, and focus on being the kind of wife *He* wants you to be. OK? OK!

Now the Lord God said, it is not good that man should be alone; I will make him a help meet suitable, adapted, and complementary for him. - Genesis 2:18

Even though help meet is two words, they are both the same and they come from the Hebrew words **azar** (aw-zar') and **ezer** (ay'zer) and mean; surround, protect, or aid.

I also looked into some reference materials and found; cooperate with, serve, side with, go to bat for, save, snatch from danger, make healthy, balm, and aid.

On the flip side, (meaning the opposite); hinder, obstruct, hold back, block, frustrate, side against, discourage, harm, hurt, injure, kill, let die, make worse.

I found this to be pretty powerful. This *completely* goes against our culture. Women want equality. We are women hear us roar!

We have thoughts like…

> *"When he does his job, I will do mine."*

> *"He should love me like Christ loves the Church."*

> *"He doesn't 'deserve' to be honored."*

> *"These are different times, the Bible was written thousands of years ago to a different culture."*

We need to realize that God is the same yesterday, today, and forever. He is *unchanging*. He does not "adapt with the times." (Hebrews 13:8) He is also not impressed by our complaining and disobedient attitudes.

He made it very clear in His Word the roles of husband and wife. We are called to be help meets, whether or not our husbands deserve it, and even if they do not perform their role properly.

God looks at each of us individually.

When we stand before Him at the end of our life, "But, Lord, He did not love me like You commanded HIM to…" will not work out, because I am **confident** that the come back from God would be…"Yes, but what did *you* do with the role I gave *you*?"

You, see ladies, it does not say <u>if</u> he does everything right. It says; "I WILL make him a help meet suitable, adapted, and complementary for him".

Guess what?

YOU are the help meet that God created for *your* husband!

God gave us His Word to help us live our lives in a way that is not only pleasing to Him, but will help *us* to have happy, well balanced lives. Yes, being your husband's, UNSELFISH protector, who cooperates with him, serves him, sides with him, goes to bat for him, saves him, snatches him from danger, and makes him healthy will ultimately make *you* happy.

How?

God's Word says so! He says we will be BLESSED!

> *So get rid of all uncleanness and the rampant outgrowth of wickedness, and in a humble, gentle, modest spirit receive and welcome the Word which implanted and rooted in your hearts contains the power to save your souls.*
>
> *But be <u>doers</u> of the Word (obey the message), and not merely listeners to it, betraying yourselves into deception by reasoning contrary to the Truth.*
>
> *For if anyone only listens to the Word without obeying it and being a doer of it, he is like a man who looks carefully at his face in a mirror;*

For he thoughtfully observes himself, and then goes off and promptly forgets what he was like.

But he who looks carefully into the faultless law, the law of liberty, and is faithful to it and perseveres in looking into it, being not a heedless listener who forgets but an active doer who obeys, he <u>shall be blessed in his doing</u> (his life of obedience). - James 1:21-25

Trust me, I am a woman who grew up in the same culture as you, and who has many of the same issues. I want you to know that I in no way claim to be a perfect wife or to have mastered all that I am going to share. I am simply a woman who loves God with all her heart and desires to be all that He created me to be as a person, mother and wife.

On my journey to find out what God's Word says about what a wife that pleases Him should look like, I focused on Proverbs 31, and discovered many treasures that I am going to share with you. Some of them may not look like treasures at first glance; however, I believe that if you open your heart and spirit to what your Daddy God wants to share from His Word, you may be pleasantly surprised.

I must warn you though...

This study will HURT your flesh when you begin to obey what God's Word says about your role as a wife. It will, at times, feel unbearable. However, press on, sisters. Do not grow weary in well doing. (Galatians 6:9) Daddy loves you and will bless you for your obedience.

Where do we begin?

The first thing that probably comes to most women's minds when they hear about the Proverbs 31 woman is; "Yeah right!"

Well, I believe it only <u>begins</u> in Proverbs 31 and that *yes*, we *can* achieve the Proverbs 31 level of greatness--with God's help!

I need you to realize that there is so much more to what the **Proverbs 31 wife** is than some unattainable picture we have in our minds. God has <u>blown me away</u> with the revelations I found in this study.

I feel that the Lord wants to really teach and minister to us on a very deep level. I believe He wants to open our eyes to HIS Truth and show us some wonderful surprises. This is an in-depth study, and we are going to dive deep into Proverbs 31:10-31, and figure out just what this woman was all about—and how we can manifest it within our marriage—in today's world.

I hope you will join me on this journey and find a better marriage at the end of it. I also pray that you put all of your hopes, dreams and desires into the loving Hands of your Lord and <u>trust Him</u> to help you along the way.

I urge you to not give up. I ask you to please take the time to read this book from cover to cover and look up all of the Scriptures. I would encourage you to stand firm on God's Word and apply *His* principals to your life and marriage. I also want you to know that this is hard. For me, personally, I fall far more than I succeed. However, I know the Truth of God's Word and I pick myself back up and keep on pressing on. I do it because I want to please my Daddy God, and be obedient to the role *He* gave me--not society. Like I said before, God does not "go with the culture of the day." He is the same yesterday, today, and forever. Isn't that comforting?

Ladies, this study is not for the faint of heart. Let us not be foolish. Instead, let us discover a new way and a new life through the truths of God's Word.

Before You Begin…

This handbook was written to engage the reader to read Scriptures and seek the Word of God for answers. It is also meant to help encourage spiritual growth. Because of this, it is meant to read one verse per day. At the end of each verse study there is a prayer and then that day's Bible Study assignments.

I pray that God Bless you, and give you the strength and courage to go against the culture to become the mighty woman HE created you to be!

EVERY WISE woman builds her house, but the foolish one tears it down with her own hands. - Proverbs 14:1

Let's Pray:

Daddy God, Thank You for Your Word. Thank You for creating me to be a woman. Thank You for creating me to be a Help Meet to my husband. Help me to let go of my flesh and worldly ideas. Help me to take You at Your Word, and not try to fit Your Word into the culture. Thank You for Your unchanging hand. Thank You for Your Love. Help me to obey Your Word. Help me to be the Help Meet You created me to be for my husband. Help me to help him shine. Help me to die to my self and not be concerned with my needs. Help me to serve my husband by serving You. Thank You. In Jesus Mighty Name, Amen.

Dig Deeper

Note: if you are doing this with a small group study, the first day, should actually be your first week. It is a time of reflection, prayer and preparation. You will need the leadership guide for more details.

If you are doing this study alone or with a study partner, then feel free to move onto day two tomorrow.

OK, onto your homework…

Answer the questions below:

What are three areas you know that you need to work on in you marriage—not what you think your husband needs to do, but what *you* can do to improve the marriage? Write them on the lines below.

servanthood
anticipating needs
patience
reverence

Now, ask God to help you with these three areas. Be open to His leading and to what *He* wants to do <u>through you</u> for the betterment of your marriage.

What are five positive things about your husband? Write at *least* 5 positive things about him on the lines below. Be as detailed as possible.

Patient, listens - Considerate
Provides - Works hard, takes care of all my needs
Great Communicator, talks to me,
Shares with me.
Amazing lover - Our sex life is
blessed and always exciting
Keeps life exciting - as he plans
trips for us as well as keeps
himself busy.

Now, praise God for those things, and remember them when
negativity, doubts and muck begins to fill your thought life about
your husband. Keep the above things at the forefront of your mind!

Love Action:

Note: each day, I will give you one assignment to do for your husband. Sometimes it will be simple, and sometimes require selflessness, other times it may seem like a repeat. Regardless...just be sure and do it!

> *From the list of 5 positive things, tell your husband thank you for at least 2 of them. Make sure that you are detailed and that he knows how much you love and appreciate him.*

Important: If you are doing this as small group study, please refer to the leadership guide for more details about handling "Love Actions" for groups studies.

Finally, spend some time praying over this study and begin to *let go of any and all that you know and believe about marriage.* Open your heart, mind and spirit to the Word and allow yourself to be teachable. Lay every thought captive under the authority of Christ and get ready for *victory* in your life and marriage!

Day 2: Proverbs 31:10

A capable, intelligent, and virtuous woman-- who is he who can find her? She is far more precious than jewels and her value is far above rubies or pearls. - Proverbs 31:10

Let's take a closer look at the word virtuous.

Webster's Dictionary defines it like this:

> 1. conforming to moral and ethical principals; morally excellent; upright.

> 2. chaste.

Unfortunately, most people read the Bible like it is a regular book. When you read the Bible that way, you may find yourself wrongly dividing it. That being said; I looked up the original Hebrew meaning of the word virtuous in this context, and guess what? The dictionary missed the mark.

The original Hebrew word used in this Scripture is:

Chayil (khah' - yil) and means; a force, an army, strength, able, substance, worthy.

WOW! That is totally different from what I have always thought. Don't get me wrong the dictionary's version is good. We should be morally upright--but, that is not what it means in this Scripture.

Now, let's reread it with the new words in place:
> *A capable, intelligent, strong, able, worthy, and a woman of substance--who is he who can find her? She is far more*

precious than jewels and her value is far above rubies or pearls.

A man with a wife that is "able" to take care of her home, is filled with substance, worthy, strong, capable, and intelligent is a blessed man.

There are a few more verses that relay the same message:

A virtuous and worthy wife [earnest and strong in character] is a crowning joy to her husband, but she who makes him ashamed is as rottenness in his bones. - Proverbs 12:4

He who finds a true wife finds a good thing and obtains favor from the Lord. - Proverbs 18:22

A wise, understanding, and prudent wife is from the Lord. - Proverbs 19:14

There is also an example of a "virtuous" woman in the Bible. Her name is Ruth.

And now, my daughter, fear not. I will do for you all you require, for all my people in the city know that you are a woman of strength, worth, bravery, and capability. - Ruth 3:11

What this tells us is that Proverbs 31:10 is describing a woman like Ruth. I encourage you to read the book of Ruth. It is only 4 chapters. You will then understand what this verse is really describing. Ruth was a strong and capable woman.

She was not your typical woman of the day. Ruth was a woman of substance. Another interesting thing about her is that she gave birth to the father of Jesse, the father of David, who was the ancestor of Jesus Christ!

Let's Pray:

Daddy God, help me to be a virtuous woman, a woman of strength, worth, bravery, capability and of substance. I want to not only be a wife pleasing to you, Lord, but I want to be a blessing to the man that you gave me. Show me Lord, in my daily life, how to make decisions that show these characteristics. Thank You Lord, for loving me, and for the power of Your Word. In Jesus Mighty Name, Amen.

Dig Deeper:

Today's Verse Focus:

> *A capable, intelligent, strong, able, worthy, and a woman of substance--who is he who can find her? She is far more precious than jewels and her value is far above rubies or pearls. - Proverbs 31:10*

Now, I would like you to read the book of Ruth. Share your thoughts and feelings about her as a woman…and wife below.

_____
_____
_____
_____
_____
_____
_____
_____
_____
_____
_____
_____
_____
_____

_____
_____
_____
_____
_____
_____
_____
_____
_____
_____
_____
_____
_____
_____
_____
_____
_____
_____

Love Action:

Do one thing today that you know your husband would appreciate that you have refused to do or only do on occasion. This can vary from cleaning something, making a favorite meal, or perhaps a task you normally do not enjoy. You know what it is. I believe God will reveal it to you during your prayer time!

Finally, take a few minutes to pray about what God revealed to you today. Ask for forgiveness if necessary.

Day 3: Proverbs 31:11

The heart of her husband trusts in her confidently and relies on and believes in her securely, so that he has no lack of honest gain or need of dishonest spoil. - Proverbs 31:11
(amplified)

And here it is in the NIV...

Her husband has full confidence in her and lacks nothing of value. - Proverbs 31:11

I looked some of these words up in my thesaurus.

Trusts and Believes: have faith in, be certain of, accept as true, swear by, put confidence in, believe, rely on, depend upon, count upon, places oneself in the hands of, accept, and look to.

Confidently and Confidence: trust, conviction, reliance, credence, convinced, certain, sure, positive, secure, and assured.

Relies: depend, feel sure of, rest, lean, place one's trust in.

Securely: absolute, firmly, bind, safe, free from danger, invulnerable, at ease.

No Lack: want, absence, neediness, deprivation, exhaustion, be caught short.

Some of these kind of go together, but, others have some pretty powerful meanings. You should reread the verse and put in the meanings that touch your heart. To be a wife that pleases the Lord, our husbands must be able to trust us.

They need to trust us with the finances that we oversee--whether it is the entire household or simply the groceries. We should be completely trustworthy in any and all areas.

I think we will stop there for today. Remember; be trustworthy in all areas as a wife. I'm sure you can think of at least several areas where Proverbs 31:11 fits into your marriage.

Let's Pray:

Daddy God, thank You for the husband that You gave me. Lord, help me to hear what was intended for me, and help me to be a wife that pleases You. Help me to be trustworthy, so that my husband will lack for nothing and have no need for dishonest gain. Forgive me, Lord, for the areas in our marriage where I have been less than trustworthy. Thank You. In Jesus Mighty Name, Amen.

Dig Deeper:

Today's Verse Focus:

> *The heart of her husband trusts in her confidently and relies on and believes in her securely, so that he has no lack of honest gain or need of dishonest spoil. - Proverbs 31:11*

Answer the questions below:

Are you a completely and totally trustworthy wife? Before you jot down yes, think about it. Are you completely honest in any and every matter no matter how big or small? Can your husband rely on you and be confident in you—in any and *all* areas? Explain your answer in detail. Share where you fail and where you succeed.

_____
_____
_____
_____
_____
_____
_____
_____
_____
_____
_____
_____
_____
_____
_____
_____
_____
_____
_____
_____
_____
_____
_____
_____
_____
_____
_____
_____
_____

Look up Proverbs 12:4. Write it out.

_____

_____

_____

_____

_____

_____

Now, write out what you feel it means for you and your marriage:

_____

_____

_____

_____

_____

_____

_____

_____

_____

_____

_____

_____

Love Action:

Get dressed, put on some make up and a casual outfit your hubby likes on you. Greet him at the door with a big smile, wet kiss and tell him how much you appreciate him working so hard! If he is not working or leaving house today, modify this by still making yourself look nice, and taking a minute to give him a warm smile, kiss and let him know how much you appreciate something about him. The goal for today is to look pretty, show affection and express appreciation for something.

Finally, take a few minutes to really pray about being trustworthy, and anything God revealed to you today. Ask for forgiveness if necessary, and help finding a spiritually, more grounded friend (who will give Biblical advice) to remain accountable with in your marriage.

Day 4: Proverbs 31:12

She comforts, encourages, and does only good as long as there is life within her. - Proverbs 31:12

Let's look at the original Hebrew meaning of the word good in this text:

towb (tobe) - best, graciously, joyful, kindness, loving, merry, pleasant, ready, and sweet.

Oh, the hidden treasures of God's Word. If we were just to read this at face value, we would miss the point being made in this Scripture.

I believe that God is trying to teach us about our <u>attitude</u> in this Scripture. When we do things with the right attitude for our husbands we are pleasing the Lord.

Think about what some of these words mean...

Graciously: pleasantly kind, benevolent, or courteous.

> Sometimes, as wives, we forget how important it is to be kind to our husbands. Some practical ways that we can show kindness are; make him a bag lunch for work, lay out his clothes, put a note of appreciation where he is sure to find it, let him unwind after work in front of the television or whatever other enjoyable activity he pursues, and/or make him breakfast in bed...just because. Also, do not dishonor him by complaining about his faults to your girlfriends. I'm sure if you ask the Lord for guidance He will help you find ways to show your husband kindness.

Joyful: glad, delighted, causing or bringing joy, and delightful.

Make the choice to do your tasks with gladness. Don't let the enemy put thoughts in your head that steal your joy. "He never, I wish he would, why can't he, when will he"... These are all garbage thoughts that are whispered in our ear by our adversary, they can also be a product of what we allow ourselves to hear, watch, etc. We must learn to rebuke them and hold every thought captive under the authority of Jesus Christ. (II Corinthians 10:5).

Loving: warmly affectionate.

Usually, it is the woman who complains about not getting enough affection. However, believe it or not--men need it too. They would probably never admit it, and I recommend you don't broach the subject with hubby. I would, however, recommend that you try it out for yourself though! Touch him, scratch his back when he's itchy, run your fingers through his hair, pat him on the rear...yes, the rear. If you have children, it is healthy for them to see that kind of affection. Nothing graphic of course, but seeing you affectionate will benefit them in their marriages.

Merry: full of cheerfulness or gaiety; joyous in disposition or spirit.

Be light, have fun! Don't make everything into an ordeal. Smile. Laugh. Seriously, a lot of times, we need to just lighten up and get over ourselves!

Pleasant: pleasing, agreeable, or enjoyable; giving pleasure.

> You don't always have to be right you know. Let him be a man.

Ready: not hesitant; willing.

> Have sex when he wants to--willingly (in your heart). This may require prayer. However, I can assure you that sex is vital for your man! Also, don't hesitate to forgive him when he is rude, selfish, inconsiderate, or just plain wrong. Be willing to adjust your schedule to accommodate his needs. He should be *first* in your life after God, of course, and before our children.

Sweet: pleasing to the ear; making an agreeable sound.

> Stop nagging him. Never yell at him. Yelling at a man is one of the worst things you can do. It is dishonoring and emasculating and you may find yourself without a husband if you do not keep your tongue in check. They are not children (even when they act like them). They are men! Respect your husband. Do not belittle him…ever…but especially not in front of his children and/or other people.

Some of you may find several of these actions hard to swallow. I know I do. But, I also know that it is only my flesh that finds it hard to swallow. Dying to the flesh can be painful and hard. We live in a world that pursues fleshly lusts and ideals. <u>We must constantly renew our minds with the Word in order to counteract society's influence.</u> The Scriptures we have gone over thus far are completely opposite from the way the world thinks and does things...

Remember, God loves you and He does not expect you to be perfect...that was the point of Jesus. He does however; want us to pursue obedience--just like any parent. He knows more than we do. So let's listen!

Let's Pray:

Daddy God, help me to be a gracious, loving, joyful, merry, pleasant, ready, and sweet wife. Show me ways that I can bless my husband and help me to see when I can do better. Lord, I want you to reach inside of me and mold me into who You created me to be. I lay all my expectations, and every area that my flesh is unhappy at Your feet. Bless my marriage, Father. Thank you. In Jesus Mighty Name, Amen.

Dig Deeper

Today's Verse Focus:

> *She comforts, encourages, and does only good as long as there is life within her. - Proverbs 31:12*

Answer the questions below:

Looking back over the descriptive words we discussed; Graciously, Joyful, Loving, Merry, Pleasant, Ready and Sweet. Which ones do you find will be most challenging?

_____
_____
_____
_____

Explain your answer:

_____
_____
_____
_____
_____
_____
_____
_____
_____
_____
_____
_____
_____
_____
_____

Look up one scripture that goes hand and hand with each of the words mentioned above. Make sure they are relevant for your situation and marriage.

You will need to use a concordance, or search engine. However, find one verse that goes with the word, and the meaning that was included in the study. You may need to go back and read them! Write out the verse on each line.

Graciously

_____
_____
_____
_____
_____
_____
_____

Joyful

_____
_____
_____
_____
_____
_____
_____
_____

Loving

_____
_____
_____
_____
_____
_____
_____
_____

Merry

_____
_____
_____
_____
_____
_____
_____
_____

Pleasant

_____
_____
_____

_____
_____
_____
_____
_____
_____

Ready

_____
_____
_____
_____
_____
_____
_____
_____

Sweet

_____
_____
_____
_____
_____
_____
_____
_____

Love Action:

Reflecting back on your weakest of the words, pick ONE and do something that shows that action.

Example: if "ready" is a weak point for you, initiate sex. Or, suggest something you do not enjoy, yet you know he does and he will <u>know</u> that you are putting him first. You can do it! I believe in you and more importantly, DADDY God does!

Finally, pray about your weak points. Ask God for help and creativity in each area. Allow Him to work in you! Also, confess any wrong and ask forgiveness where needed.

Day 5: Proverbs 31:13

I think that our study is going really well. I know this because the Lord has been challenging me in some of the areas that we have discussed. How about you?

She seeks out wool and flax and works with willing hands to develop it. - Proverbs 31:13

I had to really seek the Lord with this one. I do not make clothes. I can barely sew a button without an injury. Those of you who do make clothing for your families...WOW...I am impressed. However, there is still something for you to learn today.

We have learned from previous lessons that Scriptures are not always plain. We must dig deeper to find the real treasure. Here is what the Lord has revealed to me...

Let's leave out the first part of that Scripture...it is just one example for the point of the second half of the Scripture:

...and works with willing hands...

The original Hebrew word for willing is; **chephets** (khay'-fets), and means; pleasure, desire, delight, purpose, matter, and willingly.
Works with willing hands...

As wives, we have certain duties. They may vary from marriage to marriage. However, it is all the same.

Willing hands.

We will use house cleaning as an example simply because it is an area of struggle for me, personally. Your marriage may have a different area you should be working with willing hands—keep that in mind for this lesson. Again, I chose cleaning, because it is one of *my* issues.

We should take pleasure in our homes--no matter how simple or extravagant it may be. It should be our desire and delight to keep it looking nice. It should be done with purpose and yes, it matters!

It is very important to many husbands to have a clean house. It relieves stress and makes them feel good. Many of them need it. Those of us who struggle in the housework department, I am here to tell you that it is a flesh issue. We are in disobedience. There are no other excuses other than we are unwilling--unless, of course, you are incapacitated in some way. Your flesh has convinced you that you can't...

"It's just too much..."

"It's just too hard..."

Or, "I can't possibly catch up."

...you know the drill.

Here is The Great Physician's prescription for your housecleaning allergy:

Get over it!

I mean this with much love: Get up off the couch and say; this is the day that the Lord has made! I will rejoice and be glad in it. I will do my work as unto the Lord. I will stop being lazy today!!

In today's society, many women/mothers work outside the home. For those of you who do; I know you may not like me after this statement, however, even if you work outside the home, it is still one of your jobs as a wife. You may not want to hear that, but, it is. If your husband is helpful and takes on some, or even half of the work--great! Then, do your part with a <u>willing</u> heart. However, if your husband is not helpful, and does not feel obligated to help you, it is still *your* job to manage the home. I know this, because, Biblically, *we* are the ones that were created, by God, to be the *helpers*—<u>not</u> our husbands. They were created to *lead*.

The world says...

> *"Well, he just needs to be put in his place"*....

> *"Teach him a lesson and don't wash his clothes"*, etc.

Our flesh wants to pout and shout,

> *"NOT FAIR! I work too!"*

Yes, you do. However, your obedience to the Lord will bring you rewards in Heaven. It is not always easy to except what we consider "unfair." You should bring your anger and frustration to the Lord. He may soften your husband, and you may get some help. Or, He may not in order to build character in you. *(If he is a stay at home Dad & you are the only one who works outside the home...obviously, that is another matter, not as common, and you will need to sit down and work out a plan. Ultimately, it is between you and your husband how this situation is handled. However, it is still a source of contention, it is our jobs as wives to submit our will to our husbands—and the Lord. Hard? Yes. Fact? Indeed!)*

Moving on...

...to develop it.

Develop means: To bring out the possibilities of, bring to a more advanced, effective state. To bring into being or activity.

I'll just stop here.

Let's Pray:

Daddy God, thank You for Your Word. Thank You, that everything I need to have a blessed and happy life is right there in Your Love Letter to me. I repent of any disobedience to Your ways, and ask for Your help. Help me to do my work as unto You. Show me what my role as a wife is, and help me to be a wife with *willing* hands You created me to be. Help me to rid myself of "world made roles", and seek *Your* will for my marriage and what Your Word says my role is. Remind me when I forget...Thank You, Lord. In Jesus Mighty Name, Amen.

Dig Deeper

Today's Verse Focus:

> *She seeks out wool and flax and works with willing hands to develop it. - Proverbs 31:13*

Answer the questions below:

Did you feel anger rise up in you when I stated managing the home is part of your role as a wife? _____

If you answered yes, I would challenge you to pray about the matter, seek clarity in God's Word and realize that many times when we react angrily to correction it is because we are feeling convicted. Pray about it to know for sure.

Please keep in mind that cleaning was just an example of "willing hands". Pay attention to any and all areas that you may or may not be working with *willing* hands in your marriage.

Where do you *not* work with willing hands in your marriage? Explain in detail what it is and why.

_____
_____
_____
_____
_____
_____
_____
_____
_____
_____
_____
_____
_____
_____

Thinking about the ...to develop it... part of today's Scripture, what are your thoughts on it? How does it tie in? Explain.

Remember: *develop means; to bring out the possibilities of, bring to a more advanced, effective state. To bring into being or activity.*

_____
_____
_____
_____
_____
_____
_____

_____

_____

_____

_____

_____

_____

_____

_____

Love Action:

> *Tackle a project today that you KNOW hubby would appreciate. Big or small, it does not matter. What matters is doing it with <u>willing hands</u> and taking action so that it will happen!*

Finally, pray about any offense you may have taken on with my statements. Forgive me because this study is only intended for your good and mine! Seek God in the area of willing hands and your role as a wife, He will show you what to do.

Day 6: Proverbs 31:14

She is like the merchant ships, bringing her food from afar. - Proverbs 31:14

In the time period that this Scripture was written they did not have grocery stores. They had local vendors and merchants to buy their food from, or they grew their own. It was a rare treat to have herbs, spices, meats, and other types of edibles, from far off countries. Today, we have the local grocery store that brings the rich flavors of the world just a short drive from home.

How does this apply to us?

Well, I think the point here is that she took the time and effort to find the very best food choices for her family. She prepared good and wholesome meals for her family. Her husband was well fed.

Today, fast food French fries is a primary vegetable source in a child's diet. Why? Well, we claim because we are just too busy to cook.

Hogwash!

We need to <u>make</u> time to prepare a home cooked meal for our families. Our husbands should not have to fend for themselves because we have over-scheduled our lives with this and that.

Slow down. Cut back.

If you have kids, the most important gift you can give them is not soccer practice, flute lessons, or other busy activities--it is time with their parents and not in the car ride to point A and B. It is time sitting together as a family and eating a well made meal by Mom-- breaking bread together.

Your husband may never complain about the countless fast food meals he has eaten, and you may find a million excuses to continue your quest for a too busy life. If you have children, I guarantee you that they will suffer from lack of time with their father in a peaceful consistent family meal time. And, your husband will miss the joy of his children.

I urge those of you that this message touches to bring your schedules to the Lord in prayer. Ask Him what He thinks. You may be surprised by the answer.

Another self made obstacle: believing that you can't cook. Bologna! Yes, you can. Get a cook book and follow the directions. It is as simple as that. Start with a "simple meals" cook book and go from there.

The point is: *Stop conforming to the ideas and ways of this world. You are not of this world. The Bible says that we are aliens. (ref. 1 Chronicles 29:15 and 1 Peter 2:11) That doesn't mean live in a box, but, it does mean to make sure your ideas, goals, schedules, values, and decisions are from the Lord.*

Now, go find that dusty cook book and knock your husband's socks off with a yummy home cooked meal!

Let's Pray:

Daddy God, thank You for grocery stores, recipe exchanges and cook books. Thank you that You have made it easy for me to prepare delicious and healthy meals for my family--the family that *You* blessed me with. Help me to put forth effort in preparing meals for my family. Help me to be creative, and still stay within my budget. Show me how, Lord. In Jesus Mighty Name, Amen.

Dig Deeper

Today's Verse Focus:

>*She is like the merchant ships, bringing her food from afar.*
>*- Proverbs 31:14*

Answer the questions below:

Do you struggle with preparing meals for your family?

_____

If yes, what is keeping you from doing it?

_____
_____
_____
_____
_____
_____
_____
_____
_____
_____

What do you need to do to change this?

_____
_____
_____
_____
_____
_____
_____
_____
_____
_____
_____
_____

If you do NOT struggle with this issue, what are some ways you can still improve? Are you in a recipe rut? Reflect and explain.

_____
_____
_____
_____
_____
_____
_____
_____
_____
_____
_____
_____

Love Action:

Today is simple. Make your husband's favorite dinner and if you have kids, make their favorite lunch.

Finally, pray about your schedule if it seems too busy, or that you never have time to cook or spend down time as a family. Ask God to give you creativity in the kitchen and teach you to be a better cook--even if you are already capable. We can all improve in everything--some more than others!

Day 7: Proverbs 31:15

She rises while it is yet night and gets spiritual food for her household and assigns her maids their tasks. - Proverbs 31:15

Let's start with the beginning of this Scripture;

This is probably one of the most important qualities of a good wife. She puts her God and Savior first. She sacrifices her time and extra sleep (a big one for me) to spend time in the Word. She makes sure that she is spiritually fit, so that when her family rises, she has already prepared her heart for the day's trials and events.

As Christian women, wives, and Mothers we must stop making excuses for our lack of discipline. It is our responsibility to God, our husbands, our children, and our selves. Our priorities need to be in proper alignment.

God - Putting God first should be a priority to every Christian. He loves us and created us to have a personal relationship with Him. We must spend time in His Word for that to happen.

> *I love those who love me, and those who seek me early and diligently shall find me. - Proverbs 8:17*
> *But seek ye first the Kingdom of God, and His righteousness; and all these things shall be added unto you. - Matthew 6:3 (KJV)*
>
> *...He is a <u>rewarder</u> of those who earnestly and diligently seek Him out. - Hebrews 11:6B*

Husbands - Genesis 2:18 clearly defines our position as a help meet to our husbands. If we are not spiritually fit, we will be unable to give our husbands godly wisdom. We will only operate in our flesh. And, unfortunately, many husbands will allow a wife to lead them in the wrong direction. That is how powerful we are. It is an honorable position to be a help to your husband. Make sure you are seeking council from the Lord for your husband, and for the words you speak to him.

Children *(if applicable)* – It is very clear the importance of teaching our children about God and His ways. And, we can't do that without really knowing it ourselves. And, if they don't see you seeking Him and spending time with Him, I guarantee you neither will they.

> *Train up a child in the way he should go, and when he is old he will not depart from it. - Proverbs 22:6*

The original Hebrew word for train in this text is; **chanak** (kwah-nak') and means; initiate. The Webster's dictionary definition of initiate is; to begin, set going, or originate. To Introduce into the knowledge of...

The second part of the Scripture is:

...and assigns her maids their tasks.

I don't know too many people with maids. So, I think we need to look deeper.

This woman is obviously one who has order in her life. She is scheduled. She knows what her days hold and she prepares accordingly. She also knows how to delegate when needed. If you have children who can walk, they can help! Teach them young how to be good home managers if they are daughters, and for sons, how to be helpful husbands!!

We need to prepare ourselves for our day. Make our lists. Make lunches for the children and hubby. Be balanced. Pursue order. However, <u>SEEK the King, FIRST</u>!

Let's Pray:

Daddy God, I love you. I really love you. I want to seek your face. Help me to train myself to spend time with You, and when my flesh gets in the way, please show me. Lord, my heart's desire is to please You and know You more and more. I want my (future) children to know You. I want to be a help to my husband. Help me Lord. I cannot do this without You. I need You, Lord. I love You, Lord. You are Worthy of all that I am an all that I have! Thank you, Lord. In Jesus Mighty Name, Amen.

Dig Deeper

Today's Verse Focus:

> *She rises while it is yet night and gets spiritual food for her household and assigns her maids their tasks. - Proverbs 31:15*

Answer the questions below:

Do you have a regular time with the Lord each day?
*(Before this study)*_____

If this study is getting you in the Word more than ever before, are you willing to keep seeking God and getting into His Word daily AFTER you complete this study? _____

If your answer is no, why? If yes, how are you going to make this happen?

_____
_____
_____
_____
_____
_____
_____
_____
_____
_____

Look up Proverbs 14:1 and write it out on the lines below:

_____
_____
_____
_____
_____
_____
_____
_____

What do you think this verse is saying? Explain.

_____
_____
_____
_____
_____
_____
_____
_____

Self Reflection Time: What areas in your marriage are "weak points" where you may be acting foolish and tearing down your "own household" so to speak? Explain in detail.

Love Action:

Pray for your husband today. Specifically any temptation he may be fighting...whether known by you or not.

Finally, make sure that you take the time to do some self reflection and ask God to reveal to you any area that is not balanced. If you find an area out of balance or alignment, lay it at His Feet, and get it into proper balance/alignment. I encourage you to do this on a regular basis.

Day 8: Proverbs 31:16

She considers a new field before she buys it; with her savings she plants fruitful vines in her vineyard. - Proverbs 31:16

In the King James Bible the word fruit is used instead of "savings." The original Hebrew word for fruit in this text is; **periy** (per-ee') - and means reward.

Let's break the Scripture into 2 sections. The first section is;

She considers a new field before she buys it.

What this tells me is that she was wise with her money. She did not spend foolishly.

Are you an impulse shopper? If yes, then you do not "consider a new field" before you buy it. If you want to be a wife that pleases the Lord, then you must submit every purchase to the authority of Jesus Christ.

Ask yourself:

Do I need these new shoes?

Do I need a new blouse?

Do I need another pair of earrings?

Should I get take out? Or, should I cook a wholesome meal for my family?

The list goes on...adjust it to your own temptations to spend.

Please, don't misunderstand, I am not saying that buying a new blouse, or pair of shoes makes you a bad wife. I am saying, be frugal. Be wise with the money God gives you. Yes, by all means treat yourself, but, not every day, not on impulse, not when the money is not there, and definitely *not* with a credit card.

It is also *very* important that you and your husband are in complete agreement about your purchases. We do not need to add to any financial burdens our husbands already feel as men and providers. This is often true even for those men who have wives that work, and make as much as they do feel the burden as provider. Why? It is in their make up. It is how God created them; to provide for and protect their family.

Think about what really matters: stuff or peace. You choose.

Now, let's move to part 2;

With her savings she plants fruitful vines in her vineyard.

Remember...savings means rewards. So, when you are frugal and submit your will (spending) to the Lord...You are rewarded!

Let's go a bit deeper though...

...with her "reward" she plants fruitful vines in her vineyard.

Hmmm. Why would God want this to be there? What is He trying to tell us?

When you do His will, are wise and frugal, and you submit all financial decisions to Him: He rewards you. However, that does not mean we should take the reward and squander it foolishly. It means we should use it to plant more, and continue to be wise.

Here is an interesting fact: Do you know that most people who win the lottery spend all of it within a couple of years? They just go on a spending spree. Then poof, it's gone. God's way is far better!
He knows our fleshly nature. That is why He is always clear and thorough in His directions. He is very Wise. He is Awesome!

In closing, if you will put your faith in God, submit all of your spending (even grocery shopping) to Him, be wise and frugal: He says that He will reward you. He also tells you what to do with the reward, so that it will continue to increase.

What accountant or stock broker gives advice like that…for FREE?!

Let's Pray:

Daddy God, help me to be wise with the money that You have entrusted me with. Show me how I can be more frugal. Help me to submit my spending to You and my husband. And, Lord, when temptation comes, please help me recognize it, turn from it, and submit to Your Will. I love you Lord. Thank you for loving me. In Jesus Mighty Name, Amen.

Dig Deeper

Today's Verse Focus:

> *She considers a new field before she buys it; with her savings she plants fruitful vines in her vineyard. - Proverbs 31:16*

Answer the questions below:

Do you struggle with money? Do you find yourself spending too much or foolishly? Explain where you are at mentally--as far as money is concerned.

_____
_____
_____
_____
_____
_____
_____
_____
_____
_____
_____

Do you and your husband fight about money? _____

Did you know that more than half of divorces are rooted in money issues? Why do you think that is so?

_____
_____
_____
_____
_____
_____
_____
_____
_____
_____
_____

Find 3 Verses that have to do with money that speak to you and your marriage/life/circumstances. Write them out on the lines below.

Verse One Reference: _____

_____
_____
_____
_____
_____
_____
_____
_____

Verse Two Reference: _____

_____
_____
_____
_____
_____
_____
_____
_____

Verse Three Reference: _____

_____
_____
_____
_____
_____
_____
_____

What did you learn?

_____
_____
_____
_____
_____
_____
_____
_____
_____
_____

Love Action:

Write your husband a short love note telling him how much you love him. Tell him something you know he would like to hear in the note. Put it in his lunch, tape it to the steering wheel, put it somewhere he will for sure see it. Be creative!

Finally, start seeking God about how you use money. Ask for wisdom where needed, forgiveness where you have been unwise and help to do right. If you do not have a budget, consider making one. Make sure that you submit to God <u>and your husband</u> in the area of money. Do not put stock and hope in the material things of this world. Store up your *real* treasures!

Day 9: Proverbs 31:17

She girds herself with strength [spiritual, mental, and physical for her God-given tasks and makes her arms strong. - Proverbs 31:17

The original Hebrew words and meanings for strength and strong are...

Strength: *'owz* (oze) - force, security, majesty, praise:-boldness, loud, power.

Strong: *'amats* (aw-mats') - to be alert, steadfastly minded, prevail.

And, in the Webster's dictionary, girds means; surround

Now that we know what all these words mean, let's reread the verse:

She surrounds herself with loud, powerful, and bold praise and makes her arms prevail, and is steadfastly minded, and alert.

This woman is an over comer! She knows who she is. She is a child of the King!

I want to be this woman!

Do you?

If yes, then how?

The answer is easy, but, the *way* can be hard.

We are already over-comers. God has already equipped us with it. We just have to walk in it. All the evidence is <u>in</u> His Word!

His Word tells us who we are...

> *Deut. 28:13 - You are the head and not the tail. You are above and not beneath.*
>
> *Isaiah 54:17 - No weapon formed against you shall prosper.*
> *John 16:31 - Jesus overcame the world and its distresses for me.*
>
> *Romans 8:38 - NOTHING can separate me from God's love!*
>
> *II Cor. 9:8 - God makes all grace and favor come to me.*
>
> *Eph. 2:10 - I am the handiwork of God. Recreated in Christ Jesus.*
>
> *James 4:8 - When I get close to God...He gets close to me.*
>
> *I John 4:4 - Greater is He that is in you than he that is in the world.*

If we could only grasp what God says about us, we would find far more victories in our lives! Unfortunately, that is the hard part; knowing <u>and believing</u> what *God* says about who we are. Memorize the above Scriptures. Own them. It is the legacy that your Daddy God gave you. Your husband needs to see them *alive* in you, and If you are a Mother, then your children need to learn them as well. Teach them! Speak God's Word over them as often as possible!

Sadly, most Christians live defeated lives. But, we don't have to. The Word says;

I have set before you life and death...choose life. - Deut. 30:19

Will we go to Heaven if we live a miserable defeated life as Christians?

Sure, but why not enjoy the journey instead? Isn't that why Jesus died?? *(ref. John 10:10)*

Let's Pray:

Daddy God, thank You for giving me Your Word. Thank You for equipping me with the ability to be an over-comer in this world. Thank You that I don't have to live a defeated life. Thank You for all the wonderful things that *You* say about me. Lord, help me to remember them. Help me to choose life. I cannot do this without You, Lord. I need You. I love You, Lord. Thank You. In Jesus Mighty Name, Amen.

Dig Deeper

Today's Verse Focus:

> *She surrounds herself with loud, powerful, and bold praise and makes her arms prevail, and is steadfastly minded, and alert. - Proverbs 31:17*

Answer the questions below:

How do you think your personal spiritual condition affects your marriage?

_____

_____

_____

_____
_____
_____
_____
_____
_____
_____
_____

Do you WANT to live victoriously?? _____

Do you realize that what GOD says about you is all that matters?
_____

How has the experiences of life, the media, others, self and the world we live in affected your perception of you? Explain.

_____
_____
_____
_____
_____
_____
_____
_____
_____
_____
_____
_____

When you read what GOD says about you, how does it differ from what you have been trained by life to think?

_____
_____
_____

_____
_____
_____
_____
_____
_____
_____
_____

Now, WHO are you going to believe? The lies of the devil, experiences, self talk others and the world…OR…the KING OF KINGS??

_____

I want to encourage you again, to memorize the Scriptures from today's lesson!

Love Action:

Pray for your husbands walk today. Pray that God make Himself very real to your husband. Also, ask your husband if there is anything he needs you to pray for. When he tells you, make sure you diligently pray for the matter/thing/whatever.

Finally, seek God's Face about your *self talk*. Ask Him to show you where you are listening to lies about who you are, and anything that you are allowing in your life, thoughts, heart, mind, or ears that is causing negative to come into your thought life. Ask Him to *show you how* to live victoriously!

Day 10: Proverbs 31:18

She tastes and sees that her gain from work (with and for God) is good; her lamp does not go out, but it burns on continually through the night. - Proverbs 31:18

The original Hebrew words and meanings for taste and night are:

Tastes - *ta'am* (taw-am'): perceive

The Webster's Dictionary definition of perceive: to recognize, discern, or understand.

Night - *layelah* (lah'-yel-aw): away from the light, adversity, and season

Yesterday, we discovered that a wife that pleases the Lord is an over-comer. Today, we discover that she is not only an over comer, but she does *not* give up!

When trouble comes, her light does not go out. She doesn't throw in the towel and say; "I give up, Lord." She is a fighter! She is faithful.

She understands that adversity and trials will only last for a season.

How do you respond when you are bogged down? When there are no clear answers to your problems? Do you blame God? Do you lose hope?

To be honest with you, I have had my share of struggles. I have lost hope. There was a time in my life that I felt like God's step child. I couldn't understand why everyone else seemed to be blessed, and I wasn't. In all honesty, I still struggle with not allowing these thoughts and feelings to rise up again.

Now, I understand that God was/is molding me. We are His clay, and when you create something with clay, it must go through the fire (kiln) before it becomes a beautiful masterpiece.

I know now that I have a call on my life. My call is exactly what I am doing: helping Christian women live up to their full potential in Christ. You have a call too.

Most Christians never live up to their full potential. They allow the trials and cares of life to pull them away. They do not realize that the trials are a *reason* to be joyful!

> *Consider it wholly joyful, my brethren, whenever you are enveloped in or encounter trials of any sort or fall into various temptations. Be assured and understand that the trial and proving of your faith bring out endurance and steadfastness and patience. But let endurance and steadfastness and patience have full play and do a thorough work, so that you may be fully developed with no defects, lacking in nothing. - James 1:2-4*

Wow! These are some amazing Scriptures. I could do a whole study on these three verses alone...maybe another time.

I'm sure you understand the connection with what we are studying now. A wife that pleases the Lord keeps her joy during the trials, and does not waiver in her walk, talk, or relationship with the Lord.

Let's Pray:

Daddy God, thank You for trials. Thank You for loving me enough to take the time and interest to mold me, and form me into Your image. I love You, Lord. My heart's desire is to be a reflection of You. Help me, to remember to count it as joy during the trials that I must endure. Thank you so much for caring about me. In Jesus Mighty Name, Amen.

Dig Deeper

Today's Verse Focus:

> *She tastes and sees that her gain from work [with and for God] is good; her lamp does not go out, but it burns on continually through the night. - Proverbs 31:18*

Answer the questions below:

Look up the following verses. Write them out and then share your thoughts about each of them and how they pertain to you, your marriage and life.

I Corinthians 10:13:

_____
_____
_____
_____
_____
_____
_____
_____
_____
_____

Your Thoughts:

_____
_____
_____
_____
_____
_____
_____
_____
_____
_____

James 1:12:

_____
_____
_____
_____
_____
_____
_____
_____
_____
_____

Your Thoughts:

_____
_____
_____
_____
_____
_____
_____
_____
_____

I Peter 1:6-7:

_____
_____
_____
_____
_____
_____
_____
_____
_____
_____

Your Thoughts:

_____
_____
_____
_____
_____
_____
_____
_____
_____

Do you find yourself giving up a lot or feeling hopeless?

_____

How do you feel after this devotional?

_____
_____
_____
_____

What do you think it takes to be a woman who is steadfast?

_____

_____

_____

_____

_____

_____

Will you do what it takes?? _____

Love Action:

> *Encourage your husband today. Speak life to him all day. Watch your tongue for anything negative; criticism, complaining, arguing, speaking down, tones, etc. Be a life giver with your mouth. It can make or break your husband. Use it with wisdom!*

Finally, get into the Word. Seek Daddy's Face. Do not allow the enemy to convince you that giving up on life, your marriage or whatever is the right thing to do. *We can make it!* When you find yourself neck deep in muck, praise Daddy and press on! Find encouragement in His Word for *every* circumstance! Turn to the Lord--not chocolate, poor advice givers, bad habits or anything that is not spiritually uplifting and beneficial!

Day 11: Proverbs 31:19

She lays her hands to the spindle, and her hands hold the distaff. - Proverbs 31:19

At first, this Scripture puzzled me. I prayed, and asked the Lord to show me what it means...

This is what He gave me: As usual, if you read this Scripture the way it is written without digging deeper it appears that a wife must sew to please the Lord. Well, I sure am glad that is not what this is saying, because I can barely sew on a button.

Let's start with the original Hebrew words and meanings:

distaff - *pelek* (peh'lek): staff.

Staff comes from several Hebrew words meaning basically the same thing; **mish'an** (mish-awn'), **mish'eneth** (mish-eh'-neth), and **sha'an** (shaw-an'): they all mean support. However, **sha'an** means; support, lean, rely, rest, and stay.

I looked up support in the Webster's dictionary and it had several meanings--all very similar. The two that stood out the most were; to sustain under trial or affliction and my absolute favorite...backup or assistance in combat.

I'm sure your seeing a connection over the past couple days…

Verse 17: She is an over comer. She knows who she is.

Verse 18: She is faithful. When trials come, she does not give up, she presses on.

Now, in verse 19, we discover that she leans on the Lord. She is able to sustain under trials and affliction. She knows that He has already won the victory. She knows that she has the power of the Holy Spirit as her backup during combat. She rests in Him.

> **In Matthew 11:29-30 Jesus says;**
> *Take My yoke upon you and learn of Me, for I am gentle and humble in heart, and you will find rest for your souls. For My yoke is good - not hard, but comfortable and pleasant, and my burden is light and easy to carry.*

So, stop trying to carry it all yourself!

It may sound cliché, but it is true: we must let go, and let God!

It's like when you go to the grocery store, and you've had a very long day, you are tired and you have a ton of groceries. They are heavy. What do you do? Well, hopefully, you let the bag boy (or girl) load them into your car. It is the same concept for our life loads. Stop trying to carry all the burdens of life and lay them at the Feet of Jesus. He will carry them for you, *if* you let Him! I am sure that when you do, you will sleep better and feel better.

Let's Pray:

Daddy God, Thank You for taking on all of my burdens, hurts, and pain. Thank You, that Your yoke is easy, and that Your burden is light. Lord, I release it all to You. It's all Yours, Lord. I cannot carry these burdens (be specific) any longer. I need You to even breathe, Lord. Never leave me. Thank You. Oh, and Daddy God, when I try to pick the load back up, please don't let me. Thank You!! I love You, Jesus. You are Worthy of all of my praise. In Jesus Mighty Name, Amen.

Dig Deeper

Today's Verse Focus:

> *She lays her hands to the spindle, and her hands hold the distaff.* - Proverbs 31:19

Answer the questions below:

Do you find yourself carrying the heavy burdens of life?

_____

Are you ready to release them to the Lord? _____

I will assume your answer is YES!

Now, in order to do this properly, you will need to let go of expectations, your own desires and will. You will need to trust God in the midst of the muck and *allow* Him to take the burden and to teach you as you are walking with Him on the journey He planned for your life.

In your marriage, this means, dying to self and living for the pleasure of your Daddy God. It is not all that hard once you choose to abide in His loving arms.

Now, on the lines below, I want you to write down three things that you know you need to release to the Lord. They should be things that pertain to your *marriage*. For example, they can be: unrealistic expectations, hurts, unforgiveness, needs that are not met, etc. I am sure you know what needs to be released.

_____
_____
_____
_____
_____
_____

_____

_____

_____

_____

_____

_____

_____

_____

_____

_____

_____

_____

_____

_____

_____

Look up the following verses and write them out below.

Proverbs 3:5-6:

_____

_____

_____

_____

_____

_____

Philippians 4:6-7:

_____

_____

_____

_____

_____

_____
_____
_____
_____
_____
_____

Romans 8:28:
_____
_____
_____
_____
_____
_____
_____
_____
_____

Jeremiah 29:11:
_____
_____
_____
_____
_____
_____
_____

Psalm 13:5:
_____
_____
_____
_____
_____
_____
_____

Now, TRUST Him!

Love Action:

> *Ask God to help you rely on Him to meet your needs and not your husband. Release your husband from the burden of meeting your needs and any unrealistic expectations that you have in your marriage. Trust God with you husband and marriage. Once you do this, walk up to your husband as soon as possible (today) and plant a big, wet and not rated-G kiss on him!*

Finally, do not give up. <u>Remain strong</u>. *Know* that you *are* an overcomer and God ALREADY made the way. When you mess it all up, do *not* give up. Pick yourself up and <u>press on</u>. Keep seeking God about your expectations and pray often--more than once each day!

Day 12: Proverbs 31:20

She opens her hand to the poor, yes, she reaches out her filled hands to the needy (whether in body, mind, or spirit). - Proverbs 31:20

I'm sure we're all familiar with what the word needy means, but, I am going to give the Hebrew word and meaning anyway. We need to understand--really understand.

Needy - *'ebyown* (eb-yone'): destitute: - beggar, needy, poor.

A wife that pleases the Lord is a giver. She is ready and willing to give to those in need. She does not withhold her giving to anyone.

That seems simple enough, right? Not really. She is a true giver. Most of us are not. Let me explain...

Please note that this is not a specific person. However, there is a bit of her in all of us on some level...

Jane

Jane considers herself a nice person. She goes through her closets every few months, and bags up clothes she no longer wears. She looks around her house for items that she no longer uses. Then she takes them all down to the local Goodwill. She sure feels good about herself. She's glad she is able to help those "less fortunate" than herself. She thinks; "Why should those old clothes take up space?"

Jane gives regular offerings to her church. And every Christmas, she picks a name off that cute little tree at her local department store. She loves buying those gifts for needy little children. It sure makes her feel good inside.

This all sounds great, huh? Some of us may actually be Jane in one way or another. Don't get me wrong, this is all wonderful....

BUT...

What about that lady Jane always seems to walk by at church every Sunday? She often ponders to herself: *"Didn't she wear that dress last week? And those shoes...she really should get a new pair..."*

OR...

That same old beggar that always wants a hand out at the local coffee shop that she often rushes by disgustedly, thinking: *"He really should get a job, and for goodness sake--take a bath..."*

Do you see what is happening to us? We, the Church don't really give. Not the way God wants us to give.

God wants us to give our best! He wants us to give away our favorite dress to that lady that we know doesn't have much, not the one collecting dust in the back of the closet...

He wants us to plan to take the time and buy a sandwich for that homeless man...

He wants us to give of our time, an empathetic ear, friendship, money and intercession for those in need around us.

He wants us to give from our hearts...in love, *His* love. He wants our best. After all, He freely gave us His best.

I'm not saying don't give away those clothes that you no longer wear. Of course we should. Someone less fortunate will appreciate them. However, we should not limit our giving. We should not limit God and what He can do *through* us! Let's keep our eyes open and <u>pay attention</u> to those around us. We might be surprised at how many people need us. They may need a kind word: a couple dollars, a burger, a blanket...

In Matthew 25:42-45 Jesus says it all;

For I was hungry and you gave Me no food, I was thirsty and you gave Me no drink, I was a stranger and you did not entertain Me, I was naked and you did not clothe Me, I was sick and in prison and you did not visit Me with help and ministering care. Then they will answer, Lord, when did we see You hungry, or thirsty, or a stranger, or naked, or sick, or in prison, and did not minister to You? And He will reply to them, solemnly I declare to you, in so far as you have failed to do it for the least of these, you have failed to do it for Me.

We should not be apathetic in our attitude towards giving.

Let's Pray:

Daddy God, let this not be me. Open my eyes where I have been blind. Lord, help me to see those in need. Help me not be too busy to notice the needs of the least of these. My heart longs to please You. Show me those less fortunate than me. Show me those who need my time, love, money and prayers. Show me. Lead me, Lord, and I will obey. I will give. In Jesus Mighty Name, Amen.

Dig Deeper

Today's Verse Focus:

She opens her hand to the poor, yes, she reaches out her filled hands to the needy [whether in body, mind, or spirit].
- Proverbs 31:20

Answer the questions below:

Do you find that many times you ignore those in need of your time, money, friendship, prayers, etc? Explain.

_____

_____

_____

_____

_____

_____

_____

_____

_____

_____

_____

_____

Has your monetary giving become stale and ritualistic?

_____

Have you ever been homeless, or in extreme desperation? Explain.

_____

_____

_____

_____

_____

Have you ever needed a friend?

_____

Have you every purposely ignored someone or avoided them because you did not want to have to deal with their incessant chatter? _____

Explain.

_____
_____
_____
_____
_____
_____
_____
_____
_____
_____
_____
_____
_____
_____
_____

Do you realize that all of these missed, ignored or neglected opportunities are noticed by God? _____

How does that make you feel? Explain.

_____
_____
_____
_____
_____
_____
_____

_____

_____

_____

_____

_____

_____

_____

_____

_____

Love Action:

Do something completely and utterly selfless for your husband today. Also, pray for his giving. Ask God to reveal to him any area he is lacking in the giving department.

Finally, pray about *your* giving. Not just money. Pray about your time, money and heart. Ask God to show you where you may be apathetic, ignorant or in outright rebellion. Repent if needed. Ask Him to show you how to see others like He does.

Day 13: Proverbs 31:21

She fears not the snow for her family, for all her household are doubly clothed in scarlet. - Proverbs 31:21

She does not wait until winter to buy her family warm clothes. She has prepared for winter in advance. She lives in the present, but prepares for the future.

We need to be preparing for the future, ready for emergencies, and being good stewards with everything God blesses us with.

There are some who are blessed with an abundance of money. They are able to do more. However, even the smallest budget can accomplish much if handled properly.

> *For example: keep in mind that every little bit counts. Take a long hard look at your spending. Almost everyone has some area that they can cut back on. Even if you can only put $5 a week away most weeks, it is better than $0 dollars. Five dollars a week comes to $260 a year, and $4,680 in 18 years. It may not sound like much, but if you put it into interest bearing accounts, mutual funds, good stocks, etc. It can become significantly more in ten or even eighteen years time.*

If you take the time to find ways to save, you will be surprised at what you can come up with. And, trust me, God will bless it. He wants us to be good stewards with the money He gives us. He is like any parent, if we honor and obey Him, we will be rewarded.

Practical ways you can save money:

Groceries –

Use coupons (in newspapers, online, magazines, etc.).

Look for sales

Buy produce at a stand from a local grower (they charge a lot less than grocery stores).

Consider joining a shopping club and buy in bulk (it can save you a lot money in the long run).

Stick to your budget. If you don't have one, make one.

Take your time.

Don't just mindlessly go to the grocery store.

Have a list and stick to it!

Have purpose.

Be thrifty.

Be full! Never, ever shop hungry!

Electric Bill –

If you use the air, keep the temperature the same all day (78 degrees is perfect). Then turn it down after the sun goes down to 75ish.

Use ceiling fans.

Open your windows on breezy days and turn off the air altogether.

Open your blinds and shut off unnecessary lights.

Hang your towels and jeans on a clothesline to dry (they require more energy from the dryer).

Phone Bill –

Do you really need call waiting? Caller ID? Voice Mail? (get an answering machine)

Don't use 411, they over charge. Get up, and get the phone book.

If you have a land line and a cell phone, consider letting go of the land line and just keep the cell to save money.

Miscellaneous –

Make your husband a bagged lunch. Not only will he appreciate the loving gesture, but you'll save money.

Stop buying lattes 3 times a week at the local coffee shop.

Stop using your credit cards. The interest...eeek.

Don't spend more than you make.

Stop trying to keep up with the Jones'.

Create a budget and STICK to it!

PRAY before you spend!

I'm sure if you sit and think, you can come up with tons of ways to save money. Some of these suggestions may work for you...some may not. The point is, we can all prepare for our futures and our children's (if applicable) on some level. Everyone has something to bring to the table.

I just want to say in closing; I know what it is like to feel like you never have enough. I have lived it. I still do! It is very hard. It can be extremely discouraging. I also know that it only lasts for a season. God is a rewarder to those who diligently seek Him. If you seek Him and His Kingdom, He will bless you with all the other "stuff" as *His* Will sees fit for your life. Whatever He does not give us, I am certain is for our own good! *Daddy knows BEST!*

Let's Pray:

Daddy God, help me to be thrifty. Help me to be a good steward with the money you give me. Help me to prepare for my future and my children's future. Show me where I can cut back. Help me to put the needs of my husband (and family) before my own desires. Help me to do Your will with all that I am, and all that I have. Thank You, Lord. In Jesus Mighty Name, Amen.

Dig Deeper

Today's Verse Focus:

> *She fears not the snow for her family, for all her household are doubly clothed in scarlet. - Proverbs 31:21*

Answer the questions below:

Do you have a budget that you actually stick to?

_____

If not, why?

_____

_____

_____

_____

_____

_____

Are you preparing for your future? _____

Explain.

_____

_____

_____

_____

_____

_____

_____

_____

_____

_____

_____

_____

What are some practical ways you can cut back on spending and be a better steward with what God has given you?

_____

_____

_____

_____

_____

_____
_____
_____
_____
_____
_____
_____

Now, will you implement them?? _____

Look up 3 Scriptures that talk about being WISE with money.
Write them below…

Verse One Reference:

_____

Scripture:

_____
_____
_____
_____
_____
_____
_____
_____
_____
_____
_____
_____

Verse Two Reference:

_____

Scripture:

_____
_____

_____

_____

_____

_____

_____

_____

_____

_____

_____

_____

_____

Verse Three Reference:

_____

Scripture:

_____

_____

_____

_____

_____

_____

_____

_____

_____

_____

Love Action:

Make your husband a bagged lunch today. If you already do this, make his favorite. If you never have, consider making this a habit. I am sure it will make him feel special and save you money!

Finally, seek God *before* spending money. Ask Him to guide you and help you to find ways to prepare for the future. Be willing to let go and allow your heart to be teachable!

Day 14: Proverbs 31:22

She makes for herself coverlets, cushions, and rugs of tapestry. Her clothing is of linen, pure and fine, and of purple. - Proverbs 31:22

Again, as in past verses from this study, I did not understand what God was trying to tell me.

That didn't stop me though! I believe, yet again, this is another one of those Scriptures that gives us examples of a deeper meaning.

If you are a woman who makes her own furniture coverings and rugs--my hats off to you! You are awesome! (Although, once I did make coverings for my dining room chairs...)

Anyway, I think the first part of the verse is a continuation from yesterday's lesson. However, you see, when the Bible was written it did not have chapters and verses. Man added those conveniences. That is why it is so important to pay attention to surrounding verses...

That being said, let's move on to the latter part of this Scripture.

...Her clothing is of linen, pure and fine, and of purple.

In Biblical times these types of materials were considered to be upper class. And the color purple was associated with royalty. In today's society, materials and colors are of little value.

I believe that the point of this Scripture is deeper than just colors and material. I believe that a wife who pleases the Lord dresses in an appropriate manner.

What do I mean?

Well, she does not flaunt her assets if you know what I mean. The "ta tas" are not on display for all to see. She certainly does not want her brother to stumble.

However, she does not dress like a fuddy-duddy either. She dresses her age--yet youthful and attractive. She looks good. She takes care of herself. She fixes her hair and puts on a bit of makeup when appropriate.

Those of us that are full time Mothers, taking the time to look good is no easy task! There are days I try to remember if I even brushed my teeth. My husband has come home to a woman that looked nothing like the one he married.

We should take care of ourselves. God made us feminine. He made us to be pretty. Our husbands should come home to an attractive wife. I don't mean we have to look like the cover of a magazine. However, we could brush our hair and teeth. Put a little powder on. Dab on some perfume and deodorant. And, put some presentable clothes on. Not only will our husbands appreciate it, but our children (for those of us with them) should see it modeled before them.

In our current culture, women have taken on many masculine styles and hair do's. God created us feminine and we should celebrate that. I'm not saying it's sinful to have short hair and wear jeans. I'm saying; be *feminine* in whatever you wear!

Some ways a woman can enhance her femininity:

Get our hair done at least every other month. It's OK to get a hair cut.

Paint your fingernails and toenails.

Scrub those calloused heels.

Wear jewelry...even a pretty watch.

Take care of our skin. Buy some good quality cleanser and creams. Use them.

Wear dresses a little more (if you don't already)

Buy some sexy under clothes (make sure your hubby notices)

Wear perfume and scented lotions.

Lose the extra pounds. You <u>can</u> and you <u>should</u>! No excuses, ladies! God convicted me BIG time with this! We need to be balanced in <u>all</u> areas of our lives--including our eating habits!

I'm sure there are *many* more things you can think of.

The bottom line is: *We were <u>created by God as females</u>. Let's look and smell the part.*

If we are Mothers: our daughters should know how to be feminine, and our sons should know what a female is supposed to look like.

I know life gets busy--make the time. You'll be glad you did. Your children will be glad you did and your husband will be *really* glad you did.

In closing and I am sorry to be so blunt…

It is naïve to think your husband will have the desire/will-power to remain faithful with his eyes if his wife, the woman he married and chose to spend his life with, refuses to take the time to look good! He will be more likely to stumble in this area. Everywhere the man goes there are images of attractive women. While we do not need to compete with the sinful women of the world, we can and *should* take the time to look like the women our husbands fell in love with! We should leave *no* room for the devil to tempt our husbands…

Let's Pray:

Daddy God, thank You for making me female. Thank you for the beauty of femininity. Help me to be more aware of how I look for my husband. When life gets busy, remind me to brush my hair and teeth. Lord, I love being a woman. Thank you for the woman I am. I am proud to be a woman. Help me represent femininity as *You* created it to be. Help me to raise my children to understand the differences between true femininity and masculinity so that they can be a pleasure to the one they marry! In Jesus Mighty Name, Amen.

Dig Deeper

Today's Verse Focus:

> *She makes for herself coverlets, cushions, and rugs of tapestry. Her clothing is of linen, pure and fine, and of purple. - Proverbs 31:22*

Answer the questions below:

Do you struggle with taking the time to take care of YOU?

_____

Do you think it is fair to expect your husband to not struggle even more with his eyes if you rarely take the time to look good for him? Explain your answer.

_____

_____

_____

_____

_____

_____

_____

_____

_____

_____

_____

_____

_____

_____

What are your excuses for not taking the time?

_____

_____

_____

_____

_____

_____

_____

_____

_____
_____
_____
_____
_____
_____

Do you realize that <u>you</u> are in charge of *your* schedule??

_____

Now, are you willing to be a good steward with the BODY God gave you? Are you willing to take the time to be the woman your man married? Explain.

_____
_____
_____
_____
_____
_____
_____
_____
_____
_____
_____
_____
_____
_____
_____
_____

Love Action:

Get dressed up nice and sexy. Send the kids to their grandparents, or a sitter. Create a nice, affordable, romantic night in that your husband will not soon forget! If you do not have anyone to watch your kids for the night, how about for a few hours? If all else fails, wait until they go to bed, ask hubby to meet you in the room to "talk" ... and lock the door...

Finally, praise the Lord for creating you a woman! Now, start looking and acting like one! Oh, and make sure you keep your husband so wrapped up in you (in a good/healthy way, of course!), that he does not even notice another woman!

Day 15: Proverbs 31:23

Her husband is known in the city's gates, when he sits among the elders of the Land. - Proverbs 31:23

She is a wife that tells others how great her husband is. He is known as a wise man, because he has a wife that is wise with her tongue. Her words to others about her husband are always positive and honoring.

It is *very* important to speak well of our husbands. I have known many women who speak very negatively about their husbands. Every mistake and annoying trait he has is discussed at length with anyone who will listen. I have been guilty of it myself. We like to call it "venting" or "I just needed someone to talk to." What it really should be called is sin! We are *dishonoring* our husbands.

If they do foolish things, or have aggravating qualities, we should take it to the Lord--not to our girlfriends over a cup of coffee! We should only speak words that are edifying and that will build up our husbands, not tear them down…behind their backs.

A wife should never disrespect her husband to his face either. When you are out with friends and a discussion comes up about some bad habit (or anything negative) that your friend's husband has, there is no need to chime in with what your husband does. I did this once without even realizing that it embarrassed my husband. We were all laughing. It seemed funny at the time. A month later he mentioned to me how that comment was embarrassing to him and not funny. It stung when he shared this with me. I felt so ashamed.

How many husbands never say anything? They just let those comments sting…and gradually it tears away at their egos and their spirit.

We are clearly told how we should use our tongues in many Scriptures.

Here are a couple of examples:

> *Romans 14:19 says, So let us definitely aim for and eagerly pursue what makes for harmony and for mutual up building, edification and development of one another.*

> *Ephesians 4:29 says, Let no foul or polluting language, nor evil word, nor unwholesome or worthless talk ever come out of your mouth, but only such speech that is good and beneficial to the spiritual progress of others, as is fitting to the need and occasion, that it may be a blessing and give grace to those who hear it.*

Do you want to be someone who speaks *death* over their husband's life? I don't mean you will *physically* kill him, but, you will hurt his reputation and his spirit.

> *A virtuous and worthy wife [earnest and strong in character] is a crowning joy to her husband, but she who makes him ashamed is as rottenness in his bones. - Proverbs 12:4*

Speaking negatively about your husband to others is like rottenness to his bones! Oh, Lord, may I never do this to my husband.

You may be thinking: *"He's this…and he's that,"* or *"I need to be able to talk to someone."*

This is going to sound blunt and you may even think I'm rude…

GET OVER IT!

I mean that in love. Seriously, we <u>all</u> have problems. It's time to put your big girl panties on, stop your whining and take it to the Lord. Speak some positive over your husband and focus on where *you* can improve. God is not impressed with a bunch of whining and complaining "change him Lord" prayers. He's waiting to hear you say; "change *me*, Lord."

We will find there is less to complain about if we focus on the positive in our husbands. And, focus on improving our own flaws. We have just as many as them—if not more.

Let's Pray:

Daddy God, help me to speak well of my husband. Let no unwholesome talk *ever* come out of my mouth. I want to be a crowning joy to You and my husband--not rottenness to his bones. Father, show me when I am about to slip. Help me to hold my tongue and not allow myself to let it all blurt out. And Lord, please change me. Mold me into the wife and Mother that you created me to be. Thank You, Lord. In Jesus Mighty Name, Amen.

Dig Deeper

Today's Verse Focus:

> *Her husband is known in the city's gates, when he sits among the elders of the Land.* - Proverbs 31:23

Answer the questions below:

Do you vent to your friends about your husband's flaws or anything negative? _____

Do you realize how damaging that is now?

_____

Are you going to stop? _____

Look up the following Scriptures and write them out.

Proverbs 18:21:

_____
_____
_____
_____
_____
_____
_____
_____
_____
_____
_____

James 3:3-8:

_____
_____
_____
_____
_____
_____
_____
_____
_____
_____
_____
_____
_____
_____
_____

James 1:26:

_____
_____
_____
_____
_____
_____
_____
_____
_____
_____
_____
_____
_____
_____
_____

Love Action:

Repent to the Lord if needed in this area. Then, use your tongue to speak life to your husband today. Tell him at least three things that are uplifting throughout the day. Also, ask God if you have recently used it to hurt your husband, and if the Lord reminds you of something, go to your husband and apologize.

Finally, start thinking before you speak, and do not allow yourself to use your mouth to speak anything except that which is uplifting, edifying and God-pleasing about your husband--or anyone for that matter!

Day 16: Proverbs 31:24

She makes fine linen garments and leads others to buy them; she delivers to the merchants girdles. - Proverbs 31:24

She is an entrepreneur. She is wise to use her skills to earn some extra money.

God has given each of us a talent (some more than one). You may have the ability to bake the greatest cookies, sew, write, organize, cook, clean, make crafts, web design, teach, hospitality, etc. We should be wise with our God given talents and use them.

The woman in this Scripture had the ability to sew very well. She then used that God-given talent to create a "business" for herself. She was a good steward and used her talent to bless her family.

Are we using our God-given talents?

Well, I can only speak for myself. Honestly, I have only just begun to use the talent that God has given me. I wish I would have started earlier...

No matter what your talent is (and yes, you do have one), use it wisely. Learn it. Master it. Investigate it. Use it. You can create a small business or maybe just some side income. At the very least use it for enjoyment.

Our talents can be used to bring glory to our Lord, share His Truth, bless our family financially, bless others, and so much more! We should never waste what God gives us. It was given to us for a reason and should be used! Don't waste it. Pray for guidance and jump in!

Let me leave you with this...

"Again, the Kingdom of Heaven can be illustrated by the story of a man going on a long trip. He called together his servants and entrusted his money to them while he was gone.

He gave five bags of silver to one, two bags of silver to another and one bag of silver to the last—dividing it in proportion to their abilities. He then left on his trip.

"The servant who received the five bags of silver began to invest the money and earned five more.

The servant with two bags of silver also went to work and earned two more.

But the servant who received the one bag of silver dug a hole in the ground and hid the master's money.

"After a long time their master returned from his trip and called them to give an account of how they had used his money.

The servant to whom he had entrusted the five bags of silver came forward with five more and said, 'Master, you gave me five bags of silver to invest, and I have earned five more.'

"The master was full of praise. 'Well done, my good and faithful servant. You have been faithful in handling this small amount, so now I will give you many more responsibilities. Let's celebrate together!'
"The servant who had received the two bags of silver came forward and said, 'Master, you gave me two bags of silver to invest, and I have earned two more.'

"The master said, 'Well done, my good and faithful servant. You have been faithful in handling this small amount, so now I will give you many more responsibilities. Let's celebrate together!'

"Then the servant with the one bag of silver came and said, 'Master, I knew you were a harsh man, harvesting crops you didn't plant and gathering crops you didn't cultivate. I was afraid I would lose your money, so I hid it in the earth. Look, here is your money back.'

"But the master replied, 'You wicked and lazy servant! If you knew I harvested crops I didn't plant and gathered crops I didn't cultivate, why didn't you deposit my money in the bank? At least I could have gotten some interest on it.'

"Then he ordered, 'Take the money from this servant, and give it to the one with the ten bags of silver.

To those who use well what they are given, even more will be given, and they will have abundance. But from those who do nothing, even what little they have will be taken away.

Now throw this useless servant into outer darkness, where there will be weeping and gnashing of teeth.' - Matthew 25:14-30

What did God give you??

Let's Pray:

Daddy God, help me to see and use the talents You have given me. Help me to not waste the gifts You have placed within me. Show me how I can honor You and my husband; earn income, help others, or whatever YOU desire with my talent. Father, help me bring glory to your Name by *using* the talents that You have given me. Thank You, Lord. In Jesus Mighty Name, Amen.

Dig Deeper

Today's Verse Focus:

> *She makes fine linen garments and leads others to buy them; she delivers to the merchants girdles. - Proverbs 31:24*

Answer the questions below:

Meditate on the Scriptures I gave you in Matthew 25:14-30. What did you think of the parable?

_____

_____

_____

_____

_____

_____

_____

_____

_____

_____

_____

_____

_____

_____

Are you using your talents? Explain.

_____
_____
_____
_____
_____
_____
_____
_____
_____
_____
_____
_____
_____

Love Action:

I want you to do the same thing you did yesterday: Use your tongue to speak life to your husband today. Tell him at least three things that are uplifting throughout the day.

Note: Always make sure that what you are doing has been prayed over and <u>will not bring disunity into the marriage</u>. Your husband's thoughts and needs matter and must be valued. God's will is <u>not</u> for a marriage to end over a talent—or for there to be enough discord from it that it harms the marriage!

Finally, ask God to help you see your worth for His Kingdom. If you know what your talents are; ask Him to show you how/where/when to use them. If you do not know, ASK Him to reveal it to you! He WILL! I am certain!

Day 17: Proverbs 31:25

Strength and honor are her clothing and her position is strong and secure. She rejoices over the future. - Proverbs 31:25

Let's look at a few words in their original Hebrew before we begin.

Strength - *owz* (oze): boldness, power, might, strong, security, praise.

Honor - *hadar* (haw-dawr'): magnificence, excellence.

Rejoices - *sachaq* (saw-khak'): laugh (in pleasure).

She has no worries. She *knows* that God is in control of her life and destiny. She knows because *she* put Him in charge.

Many women struggle with the control factor. We are so used to being in charge of our homes, children, family, work, etc. We sometimes have a hard time trusting God with our worries, anxieties, futures, husbands, children, and ourselves. We want everything fixed and perfect. We want it all laid out. We want to know.

Unfortunately, that is not the way God works. He wants us to trust Him with all of it.

Our Children (if applicable)**:** God wants us to do our best to train them up the way He taught us in His Word. Then, He wants us to let go, and trust Him to handle the rest.

Our Husbands: God wants us to respect and serve them. He wants us to put them first (after Him, of course). He wants us to pray unselfishly for them. Not for our benefit, but for theirs. Finally, He wants us to <u>let go of all of our expectations</u> and trust Him with our husbands.

We do the best we can. I mean, the very best we can to be obedient to the Will of God. Then, we put all of our trust in Him. We may not get everything we want; however, we will most certainly have peace.

Just look at what the Scriptures tell us...

> *Psalm 62:8 - Trust in, lean on, rely on, and have confidence in Him at all times, you people; pour out your hearts before Him. God is a refuge for us (a fortress and a high tower).*

> *Psalm 84:12 - O Lord of hosts, blessed (happy, fortunate, to be envied) is the man who trusts in You, committing all and confidently looking to You without fear or misgiving!*

> *Isaiah 26:4 - Trust in the Lord (commit yourself to Him, lean on Him, hope confidently in Him) forever; for the Lord God is an everlasting Rock (the Rock of Ages)*

> *Jeremiah 17: 7-8 - Blessed is the man who believes in, and relies on the Lord, and whose hope and confidence the Lord is. For he shall be like a tree planted by the waters that spreads out its roots by the river; and it shall not see and fear when heat comes; but its leaf shall be green. It shall not be anxious and full of care in the year of drought, nor shall it cease yielding fruit.*

Wow! That should be enough to make us want to trust in our Daddy God. But, just in case...

> *Proverbs 3:5-6 - Lean on, trust in, and be confident in the Lord with all of your heart and mind and do not rely on*

your own insight or understanding. In all your ways acknowledge him, and He will direct and make straight and plain your paths.

Isaiah 12:2 - Behold, God, my salvation! I will trust and not be afraid, for the Lord God is my strength and song; yes, he has become my salvation. ***(I highly recommend reading this very short chapter.)***

There are many more verses that encourage us to trust in our trustworthy God. If you need more, look up "trust" in the back of your Bible. You'll be amazed!

Bottom line: *Stop worrying and fretting. Whatever your troubles are, take them to the Lord. More importantly, <u>leave them there</u>!*

Let's Pray:

Daddy God, Thank You for being my Rock. Thank You for being my support and very present help in time of need. Lord, I ask that You help me to put all of my trust in You. I know that You are trustworthy. Daddy God, I cannot hold on to my junk any longer. Please take it from me. I trust You with my life, my children's lives, my husband's life, and everything and everyone I love. Thank You, Lord for loving me. In Jesus Mighty Name, Amen.

Dig Deeper

Today's Verse Focus:

> *Strength and honor are her clothing and her position is strong and secure. She rejoices over the future. - Proverbs 31:25*

Answer the questions below:

Do you struggle with trusting God? Explain.

_____
_____
_____
_____
_____
_____
_____
_____
_____

Find 3 Scriptures (different from the ones listed in the study) that encourage us to trust God.

Verse One Reference:

_____

Scripture:

_____
_____
_____
_____
_____
_____
_____
_____
_____

Verse Two Reference:

_____

Scripture:

_____
_____
_____
_____
_____
_____
_____
_____
_____
_____
_____

Verse Three Reference:

_____

Scripture:

_____
_____
_____
_____
_____
_____
_____
_____

What did these verses teach you? Explain.

_____
_____
_____
_____
_____
_____
_____
_____
_____

_____

_____

_____

_____

_____

_____

_____

_____

_____

Love Action:

> *Pray for your husband's integrity today. Ask God to convict him of any sin he is committing that could affect his integrity at work. Tell your husband that you love and appreciate him as well. When you express appreciation, do not be general. Be specific.*

Finally, trust in God. Trust Him with your hurts, desires, lost dreams, hopes, unmet needs, emotions and all of you. He is there. He wants You to bring it all before Him…and leave it with Him. *allow* Him to FILL the gaps in your life--*not* bad habits, bitterness and sorrow!

Day 18: Proverbs 31:26

She opens her mouth in skillful and godly Wisdom, and on her tongue is the law of kindness (giving counsel). - Proverbs 31:26

A wife that pleases the Lord knows that life and death are in the power of the tongue. She understands how to use it. She is careful with her words. *She thinks before she speaks.* When she does speak, it is with wisdom.

Let's dig a little deeper into some of the original Hebrew words in this verse.

Law - *torah* (to-raw'): a precept.

I looked up precept in the dictionary. It has two meanings that are relevant to this text.

> 1- A commandment or direction given as a rule of action or conduct.

> 2- An injunction as to moral conduct.

Now back to some Hebrew meanings...

Kindness - *checed* (kheh'-sed): merciful, mercy, pity

Wisdom - *chakam* (khaw-kam') or *chokmah* (khok-maw'): To be wise in mind, word, or act, exceeding, deal wisely, skilful, wit.

This Scripture is very clearly about our words (tongue).

As wives, we have a very high call on our lives. Our mouths play a very important role in the happiness and spiritual productivity of our families—and our husbands.

In Genesis, God tells us that we are helpmeets to our husbands. He created us to be a helper for them. Our mouths are the key.

I know this from my own experience as a wife. When I choose to be cranky and irritable towards my husband, or when I choose to speak unkindly towards him: I can see how it affects him. He becomes stiff, cool, detached, and unkind back. He also speaks to me less, because he is uncertain of what my reaction will be.

Now, on the other hand, when I do positive things like...

Speak kindly to him.

Respect him.

Choose to notice his good points.

Compliment his looks or actions.

Use my mouth to uplift and edify him.

...I notice he tries harder. He reaches for my hand more. He talks to me more. He wants to be the best husband he can be.

This may seem silly, but it's true. If your husband is cool and not so cozy towards you, think about how you have been talking to him lately. If you have acted more like a mother and boss towards him, why not try a new approach?

Men do not need their wives to boss and mother them. They need wives who respect them, make them feel good about themselves, share the Word with them (not in correction, but sharing), and make them feel like men, not children. If your husband is off in some area, take it to the Lord. It is most definitely *not* our jobs as wives to correct our husbands. It is God's job. If we do try to correct them, it will only bring resentment and rebellion.

We can, however, gently steer them in the right direction with our own conduct. A wife has a very strong influence in her husband's life--positively or negatively. If we spend a lot of time putting our husbands down, then our gentle persuasions will most likely only be an aggravation. However, if we make a change and start spending more time edifying our husbands, they will be more likely to listen. That is where the "deal wisely" fits nicely.

Here are several ways our words can be used wisely with our husbands...

> *Pray with him **if** he is willing.*

> *Pray for him <u>every day</u>...**especially** when you are fighting!*

> *Encourage him.*

> *Tell him how great he is.*

> *Tell him how handsome and sexy he is.*

> *Tell him how much you love him.*

> *Tell him how much you appreciate him. Be specific.*

> *Listen to him.*

All of these things should be done every day.

Let's Pray:

Daddy God, help me to be wise and kind with my mouth. Help my mouth bring glory to Your name. Help me to use my words towards my husband in a way that pleases You. Teach me how to speak. Help me to train my children up with my words and actions. Help me to set a godly example. I love You, Lord. I want to be the wife (and Mother) that You created me to be. I need You to help me. Thank You so much for loving me more than I can imagine. In Jesus Mighty Name, Amen.

Dig Deeper

Today's Verse Focus:

> *She opens her mouth in skillful and godly Wisdom, and on her tongue is the law of kindness [giving counsel]. - Proverbs 31:26*

Answer the questions below:

Do you find that most of your words are used for building or tearing down? Explain.

_____
_____
_____
_____
_____
_____
_____
_____
_____
_____

Find 3 Scriptures that deal with our tongues/words and how they affect us and others.

Verse One Reference:

_____

Scripture:

_____
_____
_____
_____
_____
_____
_____
_____
_____
_____

Verse Two Reference:

_____

Scripture:

_____
_____
_____
_____
_____
_____
_____
_____
_____
_____

Verse Three Reference:

_____

Scripture:

_____
_____
_____
_____
_____
_____
_____
_____
_____

What is one circumstance and/or situation that occurs regularly that you find will send you over the edge with your mouth. (Something that seems to consistently causes you to stumble with your mouth…specifically in regards to your husband.) Explain.

_____
_____
_____
_____
_____
_____
_____
_____
_____
_____
_____
_____

Love Action:

Say 3 affirming things to your husband today. Not all at once. Spread them out! Also, apologize for any recent ill mannered words or tongue lashings you gave him. (Recent, meaning the past 2 or 3 days)

Finally, go to God with your mouth issues. Repent of any habitual sin in the area of your words and ask for His help, guidance and conviction when you are in the midst of the muck. Keep this issue at His throne and continually be in a repentant heart, so that He can deal with you about the matter. Don't worry: Daddy is quite gentle with His baby girls!

Day 19: Proverbs 31:27, part 1

We will spend three days on verse 27.

As I mentioned in previous days, the Bible was originally written without chapter and verse. Today, we have yet another example of how verses sometimes go together. God is still on the mouth in verse 27. Hmmm... I can't imagine why...

She looks well to how things go in her household, and the bread of idleness (gossip, discontent, and self-pity) she will not eat. - Proverbs 31:27

Let's leave out what is in parenthesis (amplified translation), and read this verse at face value. It would appear to be about cleaning your house, and not being lazy, right? Well, that's why I always go deeper. I want to find the hidden treasures. Here is what I have discovered about the real meaning of this verse. The amplified version had it right, as you will see...

Household in the original Hebrew is **bavith** (bah'-yith) and means family.

I also looked up the word **idleness**. Yes, one of the meanings deals with laziness. However, one of the meanings said, of no real worth, importance, or purpose: idle talk. When I saw the idle talk, a light bulb came on. The dictionary defines **gossip** as *idle talk*. Now, I know that God is still on the mouth, for sure!

As I mentioned above, we will be spending three days on this verse.

We are going to spend one day on each of the following; gossip, discontent, and self-pity. I believe God has a lot to say to us about these three words.

Let's begin with...

Gossip

The full Webster's dictionary definition of gossip is, idle talk or rumor, esp. about the private affairs of others.

We've all done it, or at the very least listened intently to it.
We tell our children not to do it. Then they see us buy a gossip magazine at the grocery store. Or, hear us chatting on the phone with "Jane" talking about "Sandy."

We whisper in the dark to our husbands about this one and that one...

You know it's true. We all do it or have done it. We also know that it is wrong. It is unfair, hurtful, and not pleasing to our Savior.

When God was making the laws in Leviticus He knew this was a problem.

> *You shall not go up and down as a dispenser of gossip and scandal among your people... - Leviticus 19:16*

I used to love those gossip magazines. I would also be quick to listen to a juicy story about someone. God has dealt with me in this area a *lot*. I have even had to tell someone that I cannot participate in a particular conversation. I had to suggest that we talk about something else. Sure, they thought I was nuts, however, my life is not to please men. It is to please my Lord and Savior Jesus Christ! I could care less what people think about me.

The next time a friend has a story to tell of another...just say no!

Before we pray, let me leave you with the perfect verse for this subject...

> *If anyone speaks, he should do it as one speaking the very words of God. If anyone serves, he should do it with the strength God provides, so that in all things God may be praised through Jesus Christ. To Him be the glory and the power forever and ever. Amen. - I Peter 4:11*

Let's Pray:

Daddy God, thank You for Your Word. Thank You for giving me a book of instructions on how to live a life that is filled with joy and pleasing to You. Father, please help me to guard my mouth and ears from gossip. Convict me instantly when I even begin to slip. Daddy God, I do not want to be a gossiper and slanderer. Forgive me for the times that I have been. Help me keep my mouth and ears pure, so that I can be wise in my role as a wife. Thank You. In Jesus Mighty Name, Amen.

Dig Deeper

Today's Verse Focus:

> *She looks well to how things go in her household, and the bread of idleness (**gossip**, discontent, and self-pity) she will not eat. - Proverbs 31:27*

Answer the questions below:

Here are a few verses that deal with the subject of gossip and what we speak. Look them up and write them out in your own words. <u>Include any additional insights God gives you for any future need you may have on this topic!</u>

Proverbs 8:5-11

_____
_____
_____
_____
_____
_____
_____
_____
_____
_____
_____
_____
_____
_____
_____

Proverbs 11:13

_____
_____
_____
_____
_____
_____

Proverbs 16:28

_____
_____
_____
_____
_____
_____

Proverbs 17:9

_____
_____
_____
_____
_____
_____
_____
_____

Proverbs 20:19

_____
_____
_____
_____
_____
_____

Proverbs 23:16

_____
_____
_____
_____
_____
_____

James 4:11

_____
_____
_____
_____
_____
_____
_____

Love Action:

Make your husband's favorite homemade dinner and/or dessert.

Finally, read Psalm 52 *(Yes, the whole chapter)* – Use the rest of this page to add any notes or revelations you get from reading Psalm 52:

_____

_____

_____

_____

_____

_____

_____

_____

_____

_____

_____

_____

_____

_____

_____

_____

_____

_____

_____

_____

_____

_____

_____

_____

_____

_____

_____

Day 20: Proverbs 31:27, part 2

She looks well to how things go in her household, and the bread of idleness (gossip, <u>discontent</u>, and self-pity) she will not eat. - Proverbs 31:27

Discontent

Let's start with the dictionary and thesaurus...

Discontent - not content, dissatisfied, lack of contentment. A restless craving for what one does not have.

The thesaurus describes it with the following words; unhappy, regretful, bored, disgruntled, miserable, and fretful.

Content - satisfied with what one is or has, not wanting more or anything else.

The thesaurus describes it with the following words; satisfied, gratified, wanting no more, pleased, happy, comfortable, untroubled, at ease, serene, at rest, and peace.

There are two major areas that many women struggle with in the contentment department. You may struggle with both, one or maybe neither. However, from my experience, one of these two is usually a struggle area for most women.

One: discontentment with ourselves.

Two: discontentment with financial situations.
Let's look at both…

SELF

In today's society it is very hard for the average woman to feel good about herself. Splashed across the cover of every magazine is some gorgeous unobtainable body. It has been airbrushed to perfection, of course, however, we never think about that fact. Instead, we concentrate on how great *she* looks and how "not so great" we look.

Think about it...

> *We are tall...but we'd rather be short.*
>
> *We have straight hair...but we'd rather have curly hair.*
>
> *We have brown eyes...but we'd rather have blue eyes.*
>
> *We are brunettes...but we'd rather be blonde (or vise versa).*
>
> *The list goes on and on and on...*

Why are we so discontent?

Well, it all started in the Garden...

Eve was not content with all the trees God gave her. She just had to have that one tree. She was discontent. *We* are discontent.

We should love who God made us to be. He made us perfect and wonderful. He custom made us just for our husbands and we should be happy in our own skin!

> *I praise You because I am fearfully and wonderfully made; Your works are wonderful, I know that full well. - Psalm 139:14*

FINANCES

We have a car.

Are we content with that? No, we want a newer better car.

We have clothes on our backs.

Are we content with that? No, we want newer, more fashionable clothes.

We have a nice house.

Are we content with that? No, we want a bigger better house.

Whatever we have, many times we do not see the goodness of God in it, because we are too busy wanting what we don't have.

Many women (I did not say all) that work outside the home wish that they could be home with their children instead. Why do they work? In some cases, it is because they want to have a certain lifestyle. There are a lot of people who can live a comfortable life with just one income--not an extravagant one, but comfortable. They *choose* not to.

Please, don't misunderstand me, I am all for abundance. I believe God wants His children blessed.

BUT...

Not so that we can live high on the hog. Not just so that we can have a bunch of stuff. He wants us to be wealthy to <u>further His Kingdom</u>, and be a blessing to others.

He does not want us strutting around in our new leather jacket, and our brother or sister in Christ has no jacket. He does not want us eating at expensive restaurants, and our brother or sister can't make their rent, and so on...

How can we become content?

> *...for I have learned how to be content in whatever state I am. I know how to be abased and live humbly in straitened circumstances, and I know also how to enjoy plenty and live in abundance. I have learned in any and all circumstances the secret of facing every situation, whether well-fed or going hungry, having a sufficiency and enough to spare or going without and being in want. I have strength for all things in Christ Who empowers me - Philippians 4:11-13*

The Word has all the answers we need. We must choose to be content and trust God. We must have faith in Him through any and all situations. No matter what we are going through...

We have one thing that is certain: we are not going to Hell! That fabulous fact should be enough to have us dancing in the streets!

Let's Pray:

Daddy God, Thank You for all You have given me. Thank You that I have a roof over my head and food to eat. Thank You that I have electricity. Thank You for all of the blessings that I take for granted. Thank You for sending Your Son to die in my place. Help me be content in any and all circumstances. Help me be content with me and how You made me. Thank You. In Jesus Mighty Name, Amen.

Dig Deeper

Today's Verse Focus:

> *She looks well to how things go in her household, and the bread of idleness (gossip, **discontent**, and self-pity) she will not eat. - Proverbs 31:27*

Answer the questions below:

Do you struggle to be content in either of the areas of today's study? Explain in detail what and why you think it is the case.

_____
_____
_____
_____
_____
_____
_____
_____
_____
_____
_____
_____
_____
_____
_____
_____
_____
_____
_____
_____
_____
_____
_____
_____

_____

_____

_____

_____

_____

_____

_____

_____

_____

_____

_____

_____

_____

Here are a few verses that deal with the subject of contentment. Look them up and write them out <u>in your own words</u>. Include any additional insights God gives you for any future need you may have on this topic!

I Timothy 6:7-11

_____

_____

_____

_____

_____

_____

_____

_____

_____

_____

_____

_____

_____

Hebrews 13:5-6

_____
_____
_____
_____
_____
_____
_____
_____
_____

I Corinthians 10:9-10

_____
_____
_____
_____
_____
_____
_____
_____

Love Action:

Ask your husband if there is anything he needs you to do for him, then do it. Pray for his walk today as well.

Finally, never forget that you are the apple of your Daddy God's eye and He loves you very much. He made you and loves you. He wants to bless you. Be content with whatever *HE* chooses to give you in life and walk in thankfulness and contentment. Ask Him to help you and He will!

Day 21: Proverbs 31:27, part 3

She looks well to how things go in her household, and the bread of idleness (gossip, discontent, and <u>self-pity</u>) she will not eat. - Proverbs 31:27

Self-Pity

Pity - sympathetic or kindly sorrow evoked by the suffering, distress, or misfortune of another.

Self-pity - pity for oneself, esp. a self-indulgent attitude concerning one's own difficulties.

Self-indulgent - indulging one's own desires, passions, whims, etc., esp. without restraint.

Which leads us to...

Selfish - caring only or chiefly for one's self; concerned with one's own interests, welfare, etc., regardless of others.

Self-pity is something we have all indulged in:

> *Oh, poor me...*

> *Why can't I ever just get a break...*

> *Why can't I ever do this right...*

> *I'm a terrible Mother...*

> *I don't deserve to have anything...*

I'm fat...
I wish I had...

I just can't take this...

No one understands...

I would be happy, if...

Boo-hoo, poor unlovable me...

Come on, you know exactly what I'm talking about. We love to feel sorry for ourselves, especially when no one else seems to. It's really quite amusing how childish we can behave when: things don't go the way we want them to, or when we don't get what we want when we want it, or when we fail for the hundredth time.

Self-pity is nothing more than selfishness.

Self

Me...Me...Me...

It is worse than what any demon can tempt us with. It is our greatest and most vicious enemy.

Self has another name…

Flesh!

In order to overcome this mountainous problem we must die to self.

How?

When things don't go our way...

We need to remember who we are and Whose we are.

We also need to realize that whatever the problem is, it will only last a season.

Resist the temptation to feel sorry for ourselves. When we make a mistake, we don't need to feel sorry for ourselves. Instead, we need to repent and ask for forgiveness, accept and understand that God will forgive us. His Word says so.

Then, we pick ourselves up and try again!

Dealing with or flesh is VITAL to maintaining a happy and fulfilling marriage. We must get past the "me" factor and press towards what *God* wants for our lives. Until we beat our flesh into submission, we will remain discontent, unhappy, unfulfilled and ungodly wives. The *only* way to obtain peace, joy, contentment and happiness in marriage is <u>to submit to God's Word and walk in the spirit</u>.

Let's Pray:

Daddy God, thank You for Your Word. Thank You for loving me. Father, forgive me for being self-centered. Forgive me for having a fleshly attitude when things don't go my way. And Lord, help me to know that it's OK when I fail. I can run to Your loving arms and find grace and mercy. Help me get up and keep trying. Thank You for the power that lives in me. Help me to know and feel the presence of Your precious Holy Spirit. In Jesus Mighty Name, Amen.

Dig Deeper

Today's Verse Focus:

> *She looks well to how things go in her household, and the bread of idleness (gossip, discontent, and **self-pity**) she will not eat. - Proverbs 31:27*

Answer the questions below:

We need to read more on the flesh and spirit. So, even though many of us have read it...let's read Galatians chapter 5 today.

Share your thoughts, revelations and what God spoke to you while you read Galatians 5.

_____

_____

_____

_____

_____

_____

_____

_____

_____

_____

_____

_____

_____

_____

_____

_____

_____

_____

_____

_____

_____

_____
_____
_____
_____
_____
_____
_____
_____
_____
_____
_____
_____
_____
_____
_____
_____
_____
_____
_____

Love Action:

> *Thank your husband today. Think of at least three things, and then sit him down and express your thankfulness and appreciation for him and what he does. Make sure you look him in the eye and let God's love pour out of you as you speak life to him!*

Finally, lay it all down before Him. Choose to beat your flesh into submission and walk in obedience to the Lord your God.

Day 22: Proverbs 31:28a

Her children rise up and call her blessed... - Proverbs 31:28a

I am leaving out the second part of this Scripture today and we are only going to concentrate on the first part of this Scripture today. You'll see why tomorrow.

Rise - *quwm* (koom): confirm, decree, lift up, help, rouse up, stir up, and strengthen.

Blessed - *'ashar* (aw-shar') or *'asher* (aw-share'): to be straight, to be level, right, happy, to go forward, be honest, and prosper.

I looked in the thesaurus for straight and level. Here is what I found...

Straight: honest, candid, forthright, true, truthful, reliable, frank, clear, above-board, accurate, right, sound, and trustworthy.

Level: consistent.

Now that we know what these words really mean...let's re-read this verse.

> *Her children confirm, stir up, strengthen, help, and call her to be straight [above-board, accurate, and reliable], to be level [consistent], happy, to go forward, be honest, and prosper. - Proverbs 31:28*

Wow! I bet you never read it that way before. I know I haven't.

Psalm 127:3 says that children are a heritage from the Lord.

Heritage in the original Hebrew is **nachalah** (nakh-al-aw') and means: something inherited, an heirloom, an estate, portion, inheritance.

They are that and so much more. From what we have just learned from Proverbs 31:28: they are also what should push us to be honest, reliable, consistent, happy, and prosperous women.

If we, as Mothers would only realize what God intended for us, and the many blessings that come with all that being a Mother is!

Children are a true blessing from the Lord. Not only are they an inheritance--they are our motivation. They are part of our calling. If we choose to make them and what they can become a priority, we will do whatever it takes to maintain a healthy marriage before them. We will choose to be better wives, let go of selfishness and pride, and we will seek our own desires less <u>for the greater good of the family unit as a whole</u>.

If you do not have children, this is definitely something to take to heart for your future, <u>or at the very least, children in your life that you may influence</u>!

Let's Pray:

Daddy God, thank You for the hidden treasures of Your Word. Thank You for giving me a reason. Thank You for my inheritance. Thank You for my beautiful child(ren). I truly love them, Lord. Help me to remember Who loaned them to me and that they belong to You. Help me to understand why You gave them to me. Help me to be the Mother that you called me to be. Show me how to leave them a legacy of what a wife should be and what a healthy marriage should look like. Help me to live a life that pleases YOU before them. Thank You. In Jesus Mighty Name, Amen.

Dig Deeper

Today's Verse Focus:

> *Her children rise up and call her blessed... - Proverbs 31:28a*

Answer the questions below:

What are 5 things you know you need to start doing that can help your marriage? If you are a Mom, what part do the children play? If children are not a factor at this point, there are sure to still be 5 things you can start doing to help your marriage.

One

_____
_____
_____
_____
_____
_____
_____
_____
_____
_____
_____

Two

_____
_____
_____
_____
_____
_____
_____

_____

_____

_____

_____

Three

_____

_____

_____

_____

_____

_____

_____

_____

_____

_____

Four

_____

_____

_____

_____

_____

_____

_____

_____

_____

_____

Five

_____

_____

_____

_____

_____
_____
_____
_____
_____
_____
_____
_____
_____
_____

Love Action:

Put into action at least two of the five things TODAY. Then, make a decision to add on the other three in the days and weeks to come. Life is too short to put off doing the right thing. It will only leave you with regrets...

Finally, seek God about your role as a wife and Mother and the proper order that comes with this.

Day 23: Proverbs 31:28b-29

Last lesson, I left out the second half of Proverbs 31:28. The reason I did this is because the last part of verse 28 and all of verse 29 go together.

Let's get started by looking at the Scriptures in both the amplified and NIV versions...

...and her husband boasts of and praises her, saying, many daughters have done virtuously, nobly, and well (with the strength of character that is steadfast in goodness), but you excel them all. - Proverbs 31:28b-29 (amplified)

...her husband also, and he praises her: "Many women do noble things, but you surpass them all." - Proverbs 31:28b-29 (NIV)

The original Hebrew word for **virtuously** (noble) is the same as the one used in Proverbs 31:10.

Virtuously - *chayil* (khah'-yil): a force, an army, strength, able, substance, worthy.

Praises - *halal* (haw-lal'): to make show, to boast, to rave, to celebrate, commend, glory.

A wife that pleases the Lord has a husband that thinks she is awesome!

When my husband compliments me or something I've done, it makes me feel good. I like it. When he tells me I look pretty, it makes me feel pretty. When he tells me dinner was delicious, it makes me smile...

Imagine a husband who raves about his wife's cooking, raves about her as a wife and Mother, celebrates her triumphs, commends her, boasts of her, and just thinks she's the greatest thing since the invention of football.

I'm sure we all have husbands who have complimented us at least once in our marriage. For some, perhaps they receive compliments more often. However, this man was different. He was really into his wife. He was mesmerized. He was smitten. She was "it" to him.

Can we, realistically, have our husbands feel that level of admiration and respect for us? The answer is, YES…with hard work and <u>obedience to God's Word</u>!

This woman, he adored, mastered all the qualities of a Proverbs 31 wife.

Let's review...

She Is:

>*A woman of substance.*
>
>*Strong and capable.*
>
>*Trustworthy.*
>
>*Gracious, Joyful, Loving...*
>
>*Keeps a clean and orderly home.*
>
>*Cooks/prepares good meals for her family consistently.*
>
>*God is number one in her life.*

Wise with money.

An over comer.

Trusts in the Lord.

Gives her troubles to the Lord.

Generous.

Prepares for the future.

Takes care of her physical appearance.

Honors her husband with her words in public and private.

An entrepreneur.

Not swayed by the circumstances of life.

Watches her words.

Does not indulge in gossip.

Is content.

Does not indulge in self-pity.

Her children are her motivation.

All of the above qualities are what we have been studying. Obviously, we cannot become all of these things overnight. However, we should be consistently striving to be all God has called us to be. These are the qualities that Proverbs 31 has described (so far) for the wife who is pleasing to the Lord--and her husband.

I encourage you to review the areas that you struggle the most with. Use this Devotional as a reference for future review studies.

Let's Pray:

Daddy God, I love You with all of my heart. I long to please You and do Your Will. Help me to master the qualities of the woman described in Proverbs 31. I know You did not put them in Your Word by chance. Help me to become a wife that not only pleases You, but makes her husband proud. Remind me when I need a refresher. Encourage me to review the areas I need improvement in. Show me, Lord. Thank You so very much for loving me. In Jesus Mighty Name, Amen.

Dig Deeper

Today's Verse Focus:

> *...and her husband boasts of and praises her, saying, many daughters have done virtuously, nobly, and well [with the strength of character that is steadfast in goodness], but you excel them all. - Proverbs 31:28b-29*

Answer the questions below:

What areas *(from the list of qualities the Proverb's 31 wife has reviewed at the end of today's lesson)* do you find to be the most challenging?

_____
_____
_____
_____
_____
_____

_____

_____

_____

_____

_____

_____

_____

_____

_____

_____

_____

_____

_____

_____

What can you do to help make this area(s) less of a struggle?

_____

_____

_____

_____

_____

_____

_____

_____

_____

_____

_____

_____

Love Action:

*Thank God for the man He gave you as a husband.
Ask Him to help you with your struggles and teach
you through His Word how to put HIS Will for
your marriage into practice.*

*Pray for your husband's eyes. Pray that God keep
them pure and far from evil. Pray that if he has
any lust struggles that he will seek council and
overcome any temptation before it becomes sin.*

Have sex if you have not in the past 48 hours!

Finally, do not give up! Marriage is hard work, and the road to
becoming a Proverb's 31 wife can seem daunting at times,
however, with Daddy's help: ALL things are possible and you *can*
have the marriage that HE desires you to have!

Day 24: Proverbs 31:30

I am including three translations for today's verse.

Favor is deceitful, and beauty is vain: but a woman that feareth the Lord, she shall be praised. - Proverbs 31:30 (KJV)

Charm is deceptive, and beauty is fleeting; but a woman who fears the Lord is to be praised. - Proverbs 31:30 (NIV)

Charm and grace are deceptive, and beauty is vain (because it is not lasting) but a woman who reverently and worshipfully fears the Lord, she shall be praised! - Proverbs 31:30 (amplified)

All three translations have three words in common.

Let's take a look at their original Hebrew meanings...

Vain/Fleeting - *hebel* (heh'-bel) or *habel* (hab-ale'): emptiness or vanity, something transitory and unsatisfactory.

Praised - (this is the same word used as from last lesson) *halal* (haw-lal'): to make show, to boast, to rave, to celebrate, commend, glory.

Fears - *yare* (yaw-ray'): reverent:-fear, to revere, reverence.

You know me: now for the dictionary...

Reverent/Revere/Reverence - deeply respectful. To regard with respect tinged with awe. To stand in awe of. A feeling or attitude of deep respect tinged with awe. The outward manifestation of this feeling.

Transitory - not lasting, enduring, permanent, or eternal. Lasting only a short time; brief; short-lived; temporary.

Let's read it again...

Outward beauty is temporary, but a woman who deeply respects the Lord and manifests it, she shall be celebrated and commended. - Proverbs 31:30

What this means is; a wife that pleases the Lord lives her life for the Lord. Her decisions, thoughts, words, spending, routines, pleasure, and her whole life revolve around her King. She has a deep reverence for the Lord and *His* ways. She strives to live her life as an example of that. People look at her and *know* Who she belongs to. <u>They see it through the life she lives</u>.

Ask yourself these questions:

Do I really live my life for the Lord? Really?

*Do I consider Him in **<u>all</u>** of my decisions?*

Do my thoughts and words revolve around His ways?

We should think on these questions and really examine how we live our lives. Being a pew warmer on Sunday morning is not what we were called to do. We are women of God. Daughters of the King of Kings! Your life...my life...*our* lives should be a reflection of that. People should <u>see</u> Jesus in our eyes and shining through our lives.
We must acknowledge Him! Even His Word tells us this...

In all your ways know, recognize, and acknowledge Him, and He will direct and make straight your paths. - Proverbs 3:6

Even when we grocery shop...we can ask Him to help us pick a good cantaloupe or find the best deals. Just acknowledge Him. In ALL your ways.

Delight yourself in the Lord, and He will give you the desires and secret petitions of your heart. - Psalm 37:4

The above two verses alone should make you leap! By acknowledging Him and delighting in Him, He shows us where to go and gives us our hearts desire. As if sending His Son to die for us wasn't enough. He gives us much more than we deserve. My heart melts. I am so in awe of His great love for me--undeserving me.

PRAISE THE LORD! GOD IS GOOD!!

Let's Pray:

Daddy God, You are a Mighty God. You are too Wonderful for words. Your Kindness and Generosity are overwhelming. I am in awe if You. Thank You so much for calling me, and making me Yours. I love You, Lord. I want my life to reflect You. Thank You for Your love. Thank You for Your Son. Thank You. In Jesus Mighty Name, Amen.

Dig Deeper

Today's Verse Focus:

> *Outward beauty is temporary, but a woman who deeply respects the Lord and manifests it, she shall be celebrated and commended. - Proverbs 31:30*

Answer the questions below:

We need to examine our hearts today. Let's look at the questions from this study. Prayerfully answer them and seek God for clarity.

Do I really live my life for the Lord? Really? Explain.

_____
_____
_____
_____
_____
_____
_____
_____
_____
_____
_____

Do I consider Him in all of my decisions? Explain.

_____
_____
_____
_____
_____
_____
_____
_____

Do my thoughts and words revolve around His ways? Explain.

_____
_____
_____
_____
_____
_____
_____
_____
_____
_____
_____

Love Action:

Speak 3 positive things to your husband today. Try to make them things you normally do not acknowledge, have not said in awhile, or maybe never say. Prayerfully consider what the 3 positive things should be. Spread them out if possible.

Finally, please do *not* skip over today's homework. Pray about where you are at spiritually and make a decision to fix any areas that you are lacking in!

Day 25: Proverbs 31:31

Let's look at this verse in three translations as well...

Give her the fruit of her hands, and let her own works praise her in the gates. - Proverbs 31:31 (amplified)

Give her the fruit of her hands; and let her own works praise her in the gates. - Proverbs 31:31 (KJV)

Give her the reward she has earned, and let her works bring her praise at the city gate. - Proverbs 31:31 (NIV)

I love the Amplified Bible, but the NIV is my favorite translation for this verse.

In the original Hebrew the word **fruit** in this text is **periy** (per-ee') and means reward. The original word and meaning for **praise** is the same one that has been used for the past two days...**halal** (haw-lal').

This verse tells us that if we do all that we have learned, then, we will be <u>rewarded</u>. In one of our past devotionals we found out that an excellent wife gains her husbands complete trust and admiration.

Today, we learn that the last verse is a promise of God. You see, God is like any parent: When we obey, we get rewarded. This verse shows us that we get the verbal praise from others (halal) *and* the reward from God...

What does the Word say about reward?

> *Hebrews 11:6 - But without faith it is impossible to please and be satisfactory to Him. For whoever would come near to God must believe that God exists and that <u>He is a rewarder of those who diligently seek Him</u>.*

This is an important Scripture to understand. We must <u>believe</u> that He *will* reward us. He *wants* to reward us...

It can be very difficult to be a wife. It is hard to live with another person. Especially, if we don't feel appreciated or receive the affirmation, love or affection that we crave.

We can pray and pray and pray...and still never get the knight in shining armor that we feel we should have.

God loves us very much. However, He is not a genie in a bottle that we can expect to grant our every wish. Yes, He wants to reward us; however, it may not always be the way we expect it to be. It may not even be until we get to Heaven in some cases. One thing is certain though: It will *always* be what God knows we need, physically, spiritually and emotionally.

So, what do you do when you have the kind of husband who thinks he is the King of his castle and you are his servant girl?

> *Whatever your task, work at it heartily, as something done for the Lord and not men* (or husbands). *Knowing with all certainty that it is from the Lord that you will receive the inheritance which is your real reward. The One you are actually serving is the Lord. - Colossians 3:23-24*

When our husbands are difficult, and we hold our tongues, and do out tasks (their laundry, fetch a glass of iced tea, make them a delicious meal, etc.) as unto the Lord: we will receive rewards in Heaven.

The rewards that we receive in Heaven are the only ones that really matter, because they will last forever. A new car or new dress does not.

So, forget the imperfections of your husband--you know you have them too. And start doing all of your wifely duties and responsibilities with a good attitude and <u>for your Savior</u>!

Let's Pray:

Daddy God, help me to do all of my tasks as unto You. Help me to look past the imperfections of my husband and see him the way that *You* do. Sometimes, I find it very difficult to do my tasks without complaint or attitude. Please, forgive me when I fail. Please, guide me and show me where I need to change. Thank You, Lord, for the rewards that You have for me. Thank You for being the Greatest Dad a little girl like me could ever dream of. In Jesus Mighty Name, Amen.

Dig Deeper

Today's Verse Focus:

> *Give her the reward she has earned, and let her works bring her praise at the city gate. - Proverbs 31:31*

Answer the questions below:

How do you feel about today's Scripture? Explain.

_____
_____
_____
_____
_____

_____
_____
_____
_____
_____
_____
_____
_____
_____
_____

Are you willing to wait until Heaven if need be for your reward?
Explain.

_____
_____
_____
_____
_____
_____
_____
_____
_____
_____
_____
_____

Are you willing to die to your flesh and live for Christ…even if it
means you never get the knight in shining armor?

_____

If not, you need to REDO this study over and over until Daddy
gets through your think skull! Please do not take that as an insult: I
have one of the thickest!

Love Action:

Repeat the love action you had the hardest time with so far. Yes, again.

Finally, do not get your panties in a wad over silly things. Life is short. Live love, be thankful and never take one moment for granted! Trust me, when you are on your death bed, you will not be remembering how your husband forgot your birthday, or made an insensitive remark. You will wonder where the time went and how fast it flew by!

Day 26: Final Thoughts...

I hope this study has been a blessing to you. I pray that you understand this: that no matter what you are going through, no matter where you are at in your marriage, there IS hope. Our God is the Creator of the Universe and there is nothing--NOTHING beyond His ability. All He needs are willing vessels. If you are willing, He *can* perform a miracle in you that will benefit your life, husband and marriage.

Also, please know that I am praying for every person who reads this book.

I want to encourage you to pull out this book often and, maybe even consider doing this study yearly. It is important to remind ourselves of God's plan, lest we take matters into our own hands again!

Final Assignment:

Review the past few weeks, and prayerfully consider the areas that you need to work on.

Write down those areas and begin making them a priority to work on in your life.

_____

_____

_____

_____

_____

_____

_____

_____

_____

_____

_____

_____

_____

_____

_____

_____

_____

_____

_____

_____

_____

_____

_____

Love Action:

Help your husband today. Is there something he has been needing/wanting done? Or maybe he needs new socks, a back rub, home cooked meal? Whatever it is, do it for him today. Pray for him as well!

Note: Do not stop doing a daily love action. Continue to do something loving every day for your husband. It will keep your heart and mind set on good things…

Finally, do not give up! These past few weeks gave you plenty of practice to get into the Word daily. Now, you must take the bull by the horn and learn to do it on your own! Stay in the Word and I am certain you will find a lot more peace in your life, thoughts and marriage!